Surefire Strategies for Growing Your Home-Based Business

David Schaefer

Upstart Publishing Company
Specializing in Small Business Publishing
a division of Dearborn Publishing Group, Inc.

This publication is designed to provide accurate and authoritative information in regard to the subject matter covered. It is sold with the understanding that the publisher is not engaged in rendering legal, accounting, or other professional service. If legal advice or other expert assistance is required, the services of a competent professional person should be sought.

Acquisitions Editor: Danielle Egan-Miller
Managing Editor: Jack Kiburz
Interior Design: Lucy Jenkins
Cover Design: Laurel Graphx
Typesetting: Elizabeth Pitts

© 1998 by David Schaefer

Published by Upstart Publishing Company,
a division of Dearborn Financial Publishing, Inc.

All rights reserved. The text of this publication, or any part thereof, may not be reproduced in any manner whatsoever without written permission from the publisher.

Printed in the United States of America

98 99 00   10 9 8 7 6 5 4 3 2 1

Library of Congress Cataloging-in-Publication Data

Schaefer, David, 1938–
    Surefire strategies for growing your home-based business / David Schaefer.
      p. cm.
    Includes index.
    ISBN 1-57410-090-4 (pbk.)
    1. Home-based businesses—Management.   I. Title.
HD62.39.S33   1997
658'.041–dc21   97-28265
                                                                                           CIP

Upstart books are available at special quantity discounts to use as premiums and sales promotions, or for use in corporate training programs. For more information, please call the Special Sales Manager at 800-621-9621, ext. 4384, or write to Dearborn Financial Publishing, Inc., 155 N. Wacker Dr., Chicago, IL 60606-1719.

For Kurt, Kristin, and Matthew

Contents

Preface: *Lessons Learned in More Than a Decade* vii

Introduction: *Facing the Watershed Year* x

1. **Planning a Future for You and Your Business** 1
   A Home-Based Business Plan 3
   Rekindling the Fire 8

2. **Organize Your Marketing to Grow Your Business** 10
   Step 1: Evaluate Your Marketing 11
   Step 2: Turn Intentions into a Plan 13
   Step 3: Organize Your Prospects 16
   Trolling and Casting 22
   Why People Buy 23
   AIDA Is Not Just an Opera 24
   Have You Encountered These Problems Yet? 25
   Troubleshooting 27

3. **Smart Marketing Tactics Pay Dividends** 29
   Your Secret Weapon Is You—Make the Most of It 30
   12 Marketing Habits 30
   A Closer Look at Marketing "Arrows" 38

4. **Public Relations: Stealth Marketing** 47
   Tools and Techniques of the PR Trade 50

5. **Clinching the Deal: Proposals and Agreements** 61
   The Unasked Questions 62
   Sample Proposal Outline 65
   Get It in Writing: Letters of Agreement 72

v

Contents

6. Tune Up How You Charge, Bill, and Collect — 76
Are Your Rates Realistic? 77
Other Ways to Bill 80
Collecting from Clients from Hell 86

7. Make the Most of What You Earn — 91
Insurance: How Much Risk Can You Tolerate? 91
Cut Costs 94
Are You Getting All Your Tax Deductions? 95
Simplify Recordkeeping 98
Planning for the Future 101

8. Financing Your Growth and Avoiding Problems — 103
Finding Money for Growing a Business 104
Business Plans 106
When You Grow and It Shows 110

9. Get Organized — 115
Zone Your Office for Efficiency 116
Finding More Space 121
Organize Your Telecommunications 126

10. Preparing for and Surviving Rainy Days — 133
Setbacks versus Catastrophes 134
Moonlighting as a "Temp" 135
Moving to Greener Pastures 137

11. Working from Anywhere: The Mobile Office — 144

12. The Outlook for Working from Home — 153
The Futurist's View: Glen Hiemstra 154
The Researcher's View: Raymond Boggs, IDC/Link 156
The Future of Telecommuting: Gil Gordon, Consultant 158
For "Stats" Fans: Research Profiles the Home Worker 159

Appendix A: Useful Internet Addresses 161

Appendix B: Organizations for Home-Based Businesses 169

Appendix C: Starting Your Own Home-Based Business 172

Index 186

Preface

Lessons Learned in More Than a Decade

If you have found that self-employment and the home-based business can be a bumpy road, you can take some comfort in the fact that you are not alone. Here's my story.

I went into business for myself in 1984 at age 48, with two kids still in college, but close to finishing. My wife's entire salary as a teacher went to pay college costs. I had experience as a newspaper reporter, ski resort advertising and public relations director, manager of communications for one of America's largest corporations, and a hitch doing publicity and television production for a yard and garden equipment manufacturer.

I was not fired or downsized; I simply wanted to stay in Vermont and my corporate employers kept wanting me to move. So, I finally jumped ship, bought an electronic typewriter, and opened a tiny office in an old mill that was being converted to business incubator space. There, I could buy secretarial services and copying from my neighboring businesses. The first computer appeared down the hall a short time later, and I struggled to understand what it wanted me to do when it flashed "C:". Soon, I bought a fax, and rented it to the other businesses. Over the years, the lesson became: Embrace new technology, even if you don't really love it.

Every day I sent out batches of personal letters reminding everyone I knew—and others I just read about in local newspapers and magazines—that my company offered public relations and video production services. I followed up with calls and made lunch dates with the ones who sounded interested. It was easy. I began to book business and to partner with other small businesses to quote on bigger jobs. We got them. In less than a year, I had a new computer of my own and one full-time employee. Then another full-timer, a half-time secretary, and bigger and better offices. Typically, each of us had two major clients and a small project or two. It was not unusual to book two substantial clients in a week. The lesson in this phase: Nothing works better for marketing this kind of business than personal contact. No advertising is as good as lunch with a prospective client.

The next lesson was: Nothing lasts forever. Beginning with the stock market plunge in October 1987, the air went out of the balloon. Clients were often start-up businesses, highly leveraged, riding the real estate boom of the 1980s. One week the company lost four major clients; three didn't pay. Two of us went to collect from one client only to find an empty factory, with yellow squares on the office walls where the pictures had been. We followed a voice to the president's office, where a stranger was on the phone. He had been brought in by the company's overseas owners to salvage the wreckage. Get paid? Get in line. A few executives had cleaned out the checkbook and vanished.

We were failing, and it got worse. The two superb staff members, happily, made connections with larger companies and I did not have to go through the agony of laying anyone off. Alone, I spent all day marketing as the recession deepened. A core of very large businesses kept me afloat, but soon the downsizing began in the large and small alike. My corporate clients began taking buyouts and there was nobody there to replace them, so I was out, too. I had a flock of new competitors, individuals who had been bought out or let go by big business. What had been a decent portion of the business pie—our niche—was being cut into increasingly smaller pieces. Usually, the new competitors didn't last long, thanks to their corporate mentality that assumed paychecks would continue to come every week, and that business would be easy. One of my corporate clients, pondering his own buyout, told me: "What I'd really like to do when I'm out of here is maybe work three days a week and make about $100,000 a year consulting." What a concept—why didn't I think of that? (He hasn't, but still does a little consulting to get out of the house.)

Another thing happened during this same time. Larger full-service advertising agencies who once boasted they couldn't take on a client that spent less than $150,000 a year were moving down into my niche as they hit tough times. An information meeting on a $25,000 contract would turn out more than a dozen companies, including (for this little community) the biggest ones. The lesson here was: When the going gets tough, the competition gets tougher. This is a fact home-based business people must confront head on. I also learned a lot about fear.

"There's no choice; you have to sell your way out of trouble," entrepreneur Lyman Wood had once told me of his own early struggle to build a company named Garden Way. That advice became my mantra. Increasingly, though, the nature of my work had changed. There were more one-time projects and fewer long-term marketing programs. It had become more and more of a writing job—ghost writing two books, writing and producing videos, writing much of the press background material for the U.N. Earth Summit. I began showing up at the office only briefly to check the mail and chat with the neighbors. I became interested in the work-at-home trend, and finally closed up the office and moved home.

In struggling to survive the recession, I found lists that told me hundreds of things to do, but I couldn't do hundreds of things. It was returning to fundamentals that made the difference. First was taking a long view of the direction in which I wanted to take the business, an approach different from the typical business plan because it considers the intertwining of personal and business goals. Second was reducing all the advice that was being offered into four manageable categories. In fact, these are the things all businesses must do, from General Motors to those whose entire business is run from one room:

1. Create the ideal company, and keep reinventing it.
2. Provide a product or service someone wants at a price they will pay.
3. Relentlessly develop a market for your product or service.
4. Stay organized and keep records. For the solo operator, time and money are the same thing.

A few years ago I formed a partnership with two other people who also work from home now, and we have expanded into market research, work with utilities, and assist in tourism and economic development by creating regional marketing plans. So, did I snatch success from the jaws of defeat? Not yet. As I learned earlier, nothing is forever.

INTRODUCTION

Facing the Watershed Year

One of the biggest surprises for those who leave larger companies to work solo is the volatility of the home-based business. Company life was analog, linear, somewhat predictable. It was not without its problems, bureaucracy, and megalomaniac bosses, but unless the company was downsized, the paycheck came on schedule, and one could more or less live on anticipated income. Working alone from home can be a roller-coaster ride, and in a year or so it is easy to have forgotten the original goals and be scrambling for business. Like a bird of prey, you have to kill something every day to eat.

Inevitably, there is a watershed year. If you've picked up this book, you are probably in a watershed year right now. On one side is growth, on the other side, danger. Often, it comes in year two. Since 1989, the number of home-based, full-time self-employed workers has increased by about one million per year. But one of the leading researchers in the field estimates that between 4 and 6 percent of the people who start a full-time home-based business don't stick with it, so from 40,000 to 60,000 people drop out each year. Some years this number has been much, much higher.

One glimpse of this phenomenon can be found in a report completed in the early 1990s by Link Resources (now IDC/Link), which reflects a frantic search for options by people caught in the grip of massive corporate downsizing. For every eight people who started full-time home-based businesses, seven bailed out. Quoting the report:

Primary Self-Employed Homeworkers—12.2 million

Self-employment is the primary source for these homeworkers, who typically operate home businesses or freelance as consultants and contract workers. Approximately 800,000 new homeworkers began in this work style segment in 1993, but 700,000 discontinued it due primarily to natural retirement or by returning to conventional employment.

The growth in home-based businesses continues, but no one counts home-based business failures because it is nearly impossible to do so. Relatively few are incorporated, so they don't show up as business failures, and researchers only can guess if they show up in personal bankruptcy statistics. If the home business doesn't work out, people simply get a job or resign themselves to living on other sources of income.

In a recent home-based business report, Ray Boggs, IDC/Link Home Office Project Director, observed that the time of touchy-feeling experimentation is over. "Whether you are running a business from home, bringing work home from the office in the evenings, or working as a true telecommuter, you need to demonstrate meaningful performance gains." The report adds, "For those unable to resist the temptations of daytime television or chatty neighbors, the home office can be a disaster."

Even if you get through this watershed period once, it can repeat and become a cycle for the very same reasons that it is a danger in the first place. Typically, some of those "danger" factors are:

- You start fast with contacts, projects, and clients developed in former jobs. It looks easy. You don't have to work hard at marketing. Those jobs end, and there is nothing to replace them.
- Over time, 80 or 85 percent of the business will be repeat business, and another 10 percent or more will come from referrals. The fact is, you need a champion inside your client's companies. But in today's climate of downsizing and reorganization it is inevitable that you will lose your champions. For example, I did a project for a huge company that spanned from April to October, and that was to lead to a continuum of work. Between April and October, however,

all three of my client contacts were reassigned, and some even left the company. By the time the project was completed, no one was left to take ownership. Over the course of a couple of years, the turnover in large companies can have a devastating impact on your business.
- Competitors emerge. They may have a new product, a better price, better connections, and better marketing. Your business becomes "old news."
- After a period of being busy and having things relatively easy, your marketing effort has gone slack, if it ever really existed in the first place. If you had good marketing habits when you started, you may have drifted away from them. Your marketing materials begin to look tired.
- Being a work-at-home, you have slowly become reclusive or distracted. Gradually, you edge out of the business stream and are forgotten.
- You become discouraged with marketing. Rejection is hard to take, you really can't stand any more, and you quit, at least for the day. Instead of focusing on business, you paint the ceiling, run errands, or snack.
- You have run out of prospects.

Since going off to make it on my own in 1984, I have been caught in the "terrible two" trap myself, have watched it happen to others, and have been careless enough to drop my guard and let it repeat. The opposite side of the coin is to understand the nature of the watershed year, avoid it, and grow your home-based business in a direction that satisfies your financial and personal goals. Your success will be based on equal measures of vision, commitment, discipline, and agility.

You'll find the following chapters focus on these qualities. To succeed and grow, your vision of and commitment to your home-based business depend on how well it meets a peculiar blend of financial and personal goals. A home business requires you to re-evaluate how you define success. That's where Chapter 1 begins.

Many disciplines are involved in running a business from home, and one of the most important is creating a plan for your marketing and adopting the habits that will lead to consistency and follow-through. In surveys of home-based businesses, my own experience, and from conversations with others, the number one problem that the home-based business confronts is how to consistently market a service or product at a price that makes all the work and risk worthwhile. It is the second thing to tackle, after planning.

Discipline also comes into play in rethinking how you set your fees, getting organized, streamlining your work, and examining where your money is going.

Finding the money to expand, dealing with growth issues, and riding out rainy days require both discipline and agility. Your advantage is that a micro business like yours can be the most agile of all. You can build a successful business out of niches that are too small for the big mastodons.

Running your own home-based business is like an adventure play in three acts. The first act involves setting out on the adventure—a period of decision, commitment, and increasing complication. The second act is the test—a tangle of difficulties and threats. The third act involves working through the obstacles to a hopefully happy ending. Sometimes it is wonderful, sometimes it is frightening. This book is about acts two and three—taking the test and working through obstacles to get to the happy ending.

CHAPTER 1

Planning a Future for You and Your Business

> *"You've got to be very careful if you don't know where you are going, because you might not get there."*
> —Yogi Berra

*I*f your solo home-based business was working perfectly, what would it be like? How many clients would you have? What would your typical day be like? What would you *not* worry about? How close are you to that situation today?

In order to help you define your ideal home-based business, I'll share mine. I would have four long-term clients and one or two small projects. The work would be so clearly defined and organized that the same day each week would be devoted to the same one client (six or seven billable hours each day, plus time for marketing and administration). Friday morning would be devoted to smaller projects and making appointments. Friday afternoon would be set aside for cleaning up details, filing, organizing, and planning the next week. I would never have to worry about marketing or cash flow again, I could raise my rates from time to time, I could knock off early on Fridays, and I could take a vacation without feeling guilty.

That's my goal. Sometimes, it actually works out that way. By the time you have spent a year or two in business, your goals may have undergone some radical shifts that are not reflected in how you are operating. For example, at one extreme is the desire to create a new empire with your name over it and offices in New York, Paris, London, Rome, and Moscow. At the other extreme is the conclusion often reached in midlife that being in management isn't all it was cracked up to be. In fact, during corporate restructuring, midlevel managers seem to have targets pinned to their backs. You may conclude you will be happiest if you are never managed again and never have to manage anyone else, either. You'll seek the life of the "lone eagle" and create networks or virtual partnerships, but never become an employer.

If you are going to grow your business in the direction that will make you successful in the way you now define success, you need to have a clear vision of what it could and should become.

There are two kinds of planning for the home-based business: (1) business plans, which everybody tells you to do, and (2) home business planning, which nobody tells you to do but could be more important.

A *business plan* is probably what you wrote when you started your business, especially if you went to the bank for financing. Even if you didn't go to the bank, they are a good way to discipline yourself to consider all aspects of your business idea and execution. They are typical of "in the box" business thinking.

When I worked for a large company, there were dozens of people who did nothing but create spring plans, fall plans, five-year plans, product plans, staffing plans, information systems plans, and, no doubt, other plans I never saw. As head of the smallest function in a facility of 8,000 people, I got to present my plans first. I was like the warm-up act for a rock 'n' roll band. The site manager and his staff would give me an obligatory beating, and then let me go so they could bring in the people who really spent a lot of money. They were never too hard on me because I was the guy who had the budget for planning off-site management meetings in interesting places like Florida and California. In hindsight, all the planning did not always lead to good decisions. In fact, some monumental mistakes were made and 20 years later they are still fixing them.

1 / Planning a Future for You and Your Business

After the first couple of years of being on my own, I realized that for the solo, self-employed operator the planning process worked very much like company life in some ways, but was completely different in others. I wrote a business plan for my tiny venture, and my business didn't turn out to be anything like the plan. That part was similar to corporate life. The difference was that if I now made a bad decision, I had to live with it. In the corporation, I never personally felt the consequences. People forgot my plan the minute I left the room. The paycheck was automatically deposited in the bank every Monday by noon.

Working alone, I was being blown around by every wind that came through the door. The absolute necessity of bringing in business sent me scurrying in every direction.

A Home-Based Business Plan

Home business planning is different. It recognizes that home life and business are, by choice, intertwined. Home business planning integrates what you want to do with all the important parts of your life. You have made the choice that "life's work" does not separate "life" from "work."

In home business planning, you must clearly focus on a long-term direction for the business that corresponds with other goals in your life, and then identify the steps that are necessary to move in that direction. Recognize that absolute necessity and reality will still blow you off course from time to time, but if you maintain a written vision of where you are going over the long haul, you'll get there.

Once each year, usually around New Year's Day, I sit down with a notebook reserved only for setting business and personal goals. Old items that have been accomplished can be crossed off the list: courses completed, trips taken, new projects launched, equipment acquired, and so on. New items are added. I raise two questions: First, on a *typical* day 18 months from now, what do I want to be doing and what direction will the business have to take to accomplish that? Will I be working with the same kinds of clients and providing the same services or do I need to redefine my niche and scope of services? What places or learning experiences do I want to (or need to) explore in the immediate future?

Second, what will I be doing on a very *special* day 18 months from now? Possibly I'll be traveling to a special destination or enjoying the success of the new business direction. Perhaps a relationship with family or friends will have taken life in a new direction. What actions and decisions are required between now and then to make this day possible? Envisioning a day in the future is a little like rehearsing. You envision your performance in your mind's eye much like ski racers mentally rehearse their run down the slalom course.

At some point, the business and the personal intertwine, as they do in real life. I began using this imaginative process in the 1970s while still in corporate life, but restless. One of the entries from those years was, "Get out of corporate life and do something entrepreneurial." But at that time, with a young family, my planning time frame was not 18 months, it was five years. A few years ago, writing this book became an entry in the notebook. Now the notebook entries reflect the planning for a "sailing sabbatical," another dream that will never take place unless it is put on a time line. Envisioning that special day involves casting off the dock lines, pushing off, and setting a course south to Cuba. For the past three years, there have been no major acquisitions except for boating equipment.

I try to follow five steps to help me organize my goals for the future.

Step One

Imagine it is five years from today (or 18 months or ten years—your stage in life will suggest which is most appropriate). Following are some prompts to get your imagination flowing. Begin each thought with the phrase "On a *typical* day, I want to . . ."

- look out of my bedroom window first thing in the morning and see . . . (Is it what you see today?)
- say "good morning" to . . .
- have breakfast, go to _____, and spend the first two hours of the business day doing . . .
- spend the rest of the morning . . .
- have lunch (where?) with (who?) . . .

- devote the afternoon to . . .
- spend some time before the evening meal . . .
- devote a few hours in the evening to . . .

Step Two

Now try the same set of questions for a *special* or *exceptional* day and begin each thought with the phrase "On a special day, I want to . . ." If you are honest with yourself, some patterns will emerge about where you want to be, how you structure the day, and whether you are currently making progress toward or moving away from your goals. Do you want to be jumping on a plane and flying off to see an international client, or are you happy walking around the corner to your home office? Are you spending time on priorities or developing bad habits? Have you become reclusive?

Forget for a moment about material goals—the new car, new furniture, and so on—and concentrate on how you and the business will grow together.

Step Three

Establish your goals for growing. List a few specific goals in each of these six categories, or create new categories that are more appropriate to your situation:

1. *Career and business.* If the business was operating ideally, I would . . .
2. *Overall goals.* When they write my obituary, I want to be remembered for . . .
3. *Interpersonal relationships.* I could improve my relationships with (family, friends) by . . .
4. *Personal growth.* I have always wanted to take a course in, learn more about, or develop skill in . . .
5. *Enjoyment.* Just for the fun of it, I'd like to . . .
6. *Spiritual.* During difficult times, I take comfort from my belief in . . .

You are an unusual individual if by now you haven't identified at least a few major conflicts between where you hope to be going and what you are currently doing. But by identifying them, you have an opportunity to choose priorities, focus your time, and give up less important goals to focus on the most important ones.

For some reason, many people seem to be much more creative and aggressive at setting financial and business objectives than they are at setting worthwhile objectives for living with the people closest to them.

Step Four

With a focus on your long-term direction, the next step is to identify the major milestones along the way. One page in my notebook is just a list of the next 15 years, with notes that identify key events or goals. Someone enters college, someone graduates, a mortgage is paid off, a target date is set for a business milestone, it's time to sail around the world, and so on. Since the 1970s, some of my big ones have been crossed off the list: get out of corporate life and do something entrepreneurial, get involved in television production, get a book published. But I'm also still working on some important milestones that date back to 1982. Sometimes there are delays, but often the mere fact that you have a direction leads to a series of small decisions that produce surprising results. By choosing a long-term direction, you must eliminate alternatives that would lead you away from the goal. You have a compass, a guidance system that gets you back on course whenever you are blown off. Sometimes it is a small but important decision to spend the next hour doing one thing instead of another.

By now you've probably realized that this process is simply moving from the very broad to the very specific. You have begun with a long-term dream, identified major milestones, and written down some goals in the important areas. When you look at your business over the long term, it is time to consider whether or not you should focus on developing a niche market, whether your niche is expanding or shrinking, how you can expand your services or market area, if it's time for a new look, or whether you need to do some research to get a bigger picture.

Here, this kind of "out of the box" planning can be the most valuable. Suppose you decide that in ten years or 18 months you don't want to be on the treadmill of selling your time. What else could you do? Could you turn your skills or expertise into some kind of a product? What form would it take?

Well, there are many: You could consider seminars, speaking engagements, books or manuals, audiotapes, videotapes, freelance writing, a newsletter, kits of materials and instructions, niche software. How about various combinations of these products?

Step Five

Next, the goals are broken down into "to do" items. If you intend to develop a product, one goal would be to develop a classic business plan around it. Specific dates are attached to the "to do" list and woven into your daily calendar. A reasonable goal for a home business plan would be: Get my finances organized—not a goal you are likely to see in a classic business plan. The associated "to do" might be to buy and learn one of the small business checkbook or accounting computer software programs.

Who can you call today that can help you get to that day 18 months—or ten years—from now? What book could you read? What course could you take? What conference could you attend? For some mysterious reason, when you make a commitment unexpected good things happen.

I have learned over the years that this system is most effective when I set monthly deadlines for important components and post them on a wall near the door of my office. I use a large plastic planning calendar divided into months. It only contains items I want to have completed by certain dates—just a few things that I can realistically expect to accomplish—and items that are important enough not to want to mix them into the clutter of the daily "to do" list.

These are "my" items, not client timetables. Keeping these items separate, visible, and brief is the key to getting them done.

Going back through the planning notebook each year is a trip down memory lane. There will be setbacks, and you may change your mind about some things. Just don't let go of it. Reaching a dream is like learning to walk: It has to be done one step at a time.

Rekindling the Fire

Working alone, you do not have a company to structure a set of rewards and punishments for you. You forgo certificates of merit, annual reviews, cost-of-living salary increases, promotions, a corner office, the power to make people jump, and the day-to-day supervisor who makes you jump.

Instead, you will win and lose clients, fail to get paid or get paid handsomely, have to make all the tough decisions alone, and occasionally get to skip out on a nice afternoon to play.

The rejections are very personal and felt deeply. The victories may be unseen by anyone but yourself. Fear comes visiting. You spend a lot of time alone. From time to time you will hit an emotional wall. The solo, work-at-home life is not for everyone, but by now you know how hard it would be to give up your freedom.

So, structure your own set of rewards and punishments. Fear is a very powerful motivator, but not one to invite over on a permanent basis.

Once you realize that motivation comes from within, all the books, tapes, and self-help material in the world will only teach techniques that may or may not be compatible with your personality or your real goals. Therefore, I can't tell you what will work for you, but I can tell you what works for me.

First, and most important, is holding onto the dream that I talked about in the planning session. Sure, it sounds corny. But the fact that all this effort is headed in some direction, and I set the direction, is the single most important driving factor I have found. Individuals need a mission statement, if that's what a dream is called, much more than a corporation does. And it only works if it is uniquely yours, and shared by the people you are asking to live it with you. That is why the business and personal planning are intertwined. No business will ever articulate a dream of dropping anchor in a cove ringed with palm trees, but you certainly can. Taking a sabbatical to reinvent your life is a perfectly valid goal. Goals do not have to be corporate, they do not have to be conventional, they simply have to be so honestly yours that you look forward to getting up every morning and nudging them down the path. The pursuit of happiness may in fact be the happiness of pursuit.

Second, for me, is regular physical activity. I'm not an exercise nut, I just feel better physically and emotionally when my blood is full of oxygen. I do yoga every morning when I don't have to hit the road early. I walk a lot, and particularly like to walk through the woods with a notebook in which I write haikus about the seasons. Because of where I live, I can run, bike, ski, swim, or walk before settling in to work at 9 AM.

Third is trying new things that get me out of the house. Some of these are connected to business, like going to business-related workshops and events. Others are just based on curiosity about things I may once have passed by. Each winter I take some kind of course, ranging from a foreign language for travelers to natural history. Most of these excursions are tied to the long-term dream.

Finally, I like to have a trip to look forward to, particularly during our long New England winters.

From time to time, we all take a pounding, and it is hard to pick up the pieces and start over. It's a lot easier to get going if you start with a few small guaranteed successes to recharge the batteries and the sense that you are working toward that ideal day you have described.

Chapter 2

Organize Your Marketing to Grow Your Business

"Drive thy business, or it will drive thee."
—Benjamin Franklin

*N*ow that you have charted a direction for your business growth, step back for a moment and take a long view of the lessons you have learned since you started off on your own. You may have learned that some clients are a lot better than other clients, and that it's very easy to get busy and put off your marketing efforts, with unhappy consequences.

To take your business in the direction you have determined, you will need not only more clients, because inevitably some will turn over, but the right kind of clients. It is time to organize your marketing to take you toward your goals. If you don't, you may wind up scrambling for anything you can get and gradually drift farther and farther off course.

Start by looking at what you've learned so far and use it to evaluate your efforts. Then, create a marketing plan and begin to take concrete steps to implement your plan.

Step 1: Evaluate Your Marketing

Taking Stock

- Who, what, and where is your market? Where do you expect the business to come from? Will business come only from this community? This region? Nationally? Internationally? Have you been dealing with the right clients to take your business in the direction you want?
- Does your plan call for creating a niche, with business coming from one or two specific industry groups in which you have expertise, such as banks, advertising agencies, utilities, semiconductor manufacturers, or hospitals? Or will you market to a broad range of industries?
- What are the possibilities for "partnering" with other small businesses to expand the scope of offerings? Who refers clients? (For example, an accounting firm frequently refers clients to me. A business writer friend in California gets much of his business from graphic designers who need copy for annual reports.)
- What's the outlook for the clients you serve? Are their businesses healthy? Are they expanding, downsizing, threatened by foreign competition, or just holding their own? Is that a threat or an opportunity for you?
- What new prospects would take your business in the direction you would like to go? List them:

    1. _____
    2. _____
    3. _____
    4. _____

    How can you find out if these prospects are buying what you are selling? How much are they buying and who are they buying it from, if not you? (Simply call them up and ask. It may develop into new business.)
- Is what you have to offer more competitive than other suppliers? Are you up to date? Cost competitive? Can you offer the full range of what these clients need? Do you need to form strategic alliances with others to be competitive?

- Who do you know inside each company who can fill you in?
  To do: Make a lunch date with . . .
  Phone #
- What has been the impact of your marketing effort so far? What should it be? Think about your past successes and failures:
  1. My marketing has been successful when I . . .
  2. When things haven't worked out, usually it's because . . .

  Some typical problems are failure to follow up on leads and failure to go back to prospects periodically.
- What are the opportunities for new services in the market?
- What are the greatest risks in the near future? Two typical examples:
  1. I have all my eggs in one basket, and if I lose this client I'm in real trouble.
  2. My contact is being transferred or downsized, and his or her position is being consolidated under someone I don't know and who is likely to have favorite suppliers already.
- Who are your competitors? Is the situation changing? While downsizing is supposed to create opportunity for freelancers, it often creates a new crop of competitors, some of whom may be your former clients. If you are the only game in town today, and successful, rest assured your success will be recognized and soon there will be several new competitors nibbling at your piece of the pie.

Refine Your "So What"?

You've been on your own for awhile, so you know exactly what you do. But it's very easy to forget to constantly refine your description—your "marketing proposition"—and, worse, not to say it clearly and repeat it often. The following three questions will help you define your business:

1. In ten words that a high school student would understand, answer the questions: *What do I do? Who do I do it for?*

2. When people work with me, they get the following benefits . . .
3. I make my client's life or business new, different, or better because . . .

When you're asked what you do, is the answer in "1" above? Does your marketing material clearly state 1, 2, and 3? Now, can you state what you offer from the point of view of the client?

Step 2: Turn Intentions into a Plan

Now it comes down to a matter of what to do, and when to do it. Here are three techniques that work for me:

1. Lay out the entire year on a simple calendar devoted to marketing. (See Figure 2.1.) Once it is sketched out, integrate it into your daily calendar or organizer software program. But keep it handy. I keep a marketing ringbinder that includes the calendar, copies of all marketing correspondence arranged in a month-by-month chronology file, outlines for proposals and agreements, copies of mailings and lists of who received them, and several articles on marketing techniques.
2. Consider prospects on three tiers: current clients, past clients, and cold prospects who should be clients but don't realize it yet.
3. In building your calendar, try to get a handle on important timing issues. For example:
   - When do your most important prospects plan and allocate their budgets? You want to be built into next year's budget. For example, planning may be done sometime between June and August, the actual dollar amount may be approved in October, and the new funds would become available with the new year. Simply ask someone on the inside.
   - Plan personalized mailings to groups of clients and prospects in small batches that encourage you to do it rather than put it off. Shoot for three or four a year, but time them so they don't fall into the doldrums of vacation sea-

son or the pre-holiday period when no one is concentrating. Timing is everything.
- With that in mind, keep notes in your prospect database on any cycles peculiar to individual prospects. Do they match or conflict with what you're selling? Some businesses have definite cash flow swings. For example, if you are buying radio or television time, avoid pre-election and pre-holiday periods. You'll never get a discount. But in January, that's another story.

Plan publicity efforts to take advantage of editorial calendars. Many business publications have (and will give you) a calendar of their yearly editorial themes, such as banking, utilities, technology, the media, health care, and so on. Find out the deadlines for submitting material on topics related to your business, and prepare a press release or volunteer to write an article on a trend in your area of expertise. (See Chapter 4 for details.)
- Schedule follow-up activities on all your marketing efforts. When you do a mailing, plan to follow up with a call while it is on the prospect's desk and before it gets tossed into the wastebasket or filed—48 hours in most cases. Follow up with another mailing and phone call in three to four months.

The Formula for Marketing Success Is: E = MC 3+

E = Expanding your business

MC = A Marketing Communication action

3+ = At least three actions each day

Thus, your chances of growing your business are based on relentlessly initiating three marketing events every working day. Ideally, these would be three brand new marketing contacts, but to make this goal realistic and achievable, let's consider the following as "MCs":

- A cold call to a prospect on the telephone
- Scheduling a meeting with a prospect
- Meeting with a prospect
- Following up in a way that advances your chances of selling
- Sending a letter, note, or postcard to a prospect
- Attending an event where you are likely to meet prospects

In many situations, the primary objective will have to do with arranging a face-to-face meeting. Some people make their calls to self-employed prospects after 5 PM, knowing that they will be working late. Others call their corporate prospects early in the morning, before the secretary is likely to become the gatekeeper. Still others try at ten minutes to the hour, hoping to catch people between meetings. Timing is critical for success. For example, most calls on Monday morning are a waste of time because this is prime meeting time for a lot of people. I prefer making prospecting calls on Tuesday mornings because Monday is past, business is front and center, and people are in gear to do it. The weekend is not yet on the horizon.

SUREFIRE TIP

Like most people, I hate cold telephone calling, or "smiling and dialing." It's a small thing, but ending the day by looking up the telephone numbers of tomorrow's cold calls and entering them in the daily organizer eliminates one more reason not to make the call ("I can't make that call now, I don't know the number").

Thus, you come to the unhappy truth: Marketing is not really a formula at all. It is a relentless discipline, and a lack of discipline will lead first to FEAR and ultimately to DANGEROUS TERRITORY. If you truly want to grow your business, plan to spend 25 percent of every working day—that's two hours—on marketing activities. This is something to do first, not as an afterthought when you have nothing else to do, so schedule it on your daily calendar. Like a bird of prey, you must kill something every day in order to eat.

SUREFIRE TIP

Start the day with an easy call, not a tough one. Success makes me want to go forward; failure makes me want to take a nap.

The first annual calendar is the most difficult. After that, definite patterns will emerge as items repeat themselves. Keep your calendar handy and make notes. It is a constant work in progress. Remember, this is a calendar for your marketing only, not for work on behalf of clients, and not for birthdays and anniversaries.

Step 3: Organize Your Prospects

Managing marketing prospects is a detail-driven task made to order for a computer. If you've been having trouble finding new prospects, try to develop an eye for prospects the way a robin develops an eye for worms. They're all around, you just always have to be alert. Then, organize your prospect list at least once a week. It's easy to let your prospect list slip out of control, so to get back on track collect all of the

- responses to your advertising or publicity.
- referrals from other clients or business associates (the best kind).
- responses to your letters or direct mail.
- names collected while networking through business groups (e.g., business cards).
- leads from trade shows and conferences (more business cards, lists of attendees and exhibitors, and so on).
- leads from reading newspapers and magazines and clipping stories.
- names of people you know through business, social, or volunteer connections.
- names of former clients who need services in cycles but not on a continuing basis.

2 / *Organize Your Marketing to Grow Your Business* 17

FIGURE 2.1 Develop a Yearly Marketing Calendar (Revise and Update Quarterly)

January	February
Mail: "Thanks" to current clients *Mail:* Cold prospects intro letter *Phone:* Follow up new prospects mailing	*Mail PR, Advertising:* New product announcement *Phone:* Past clients on new product, make meetings
March	**April**
PR: Tourism survey results	*Mail:* All, postcard on new product
May	**June**
Phone: Follow up new product inquiries, make meetings	*Lunch:* John, Newco budget *Mail:* Brochures, our seminar
July	**August**
Phone: Current clients on budget outlooks	*PR:* Deadline, Dec. *HOC* magazine *Mail:* Seminar reminder postcard
September	**October**
Mail: All, personal new product update *Mail, PR:* Seminar	*Mail:* Research prospects on legislative issues
November	**December**
Phone: Follow up research prospects	*PR:* Deadline, "media" issues, business magazines

If you pull all these prospects together, you may end up with a shoe box full of miscellaneous pieces of paper, notes, business cards, faxes, and correspondence that all have something to do with marketing. These are the prospects you were going to follow up some day, but they were scattered here and there and you didn't get around to it. These names are the very lifeblood of your business: Some translate into business right away, some remain dormant and blossom later, some never amount to anything.

How effective is your procedure for identifying the source, tracking progress, and keeping up records on your history with each prospect and client? If the system is a good one, have you been keeping it up to date or did you make one attempt at marketing and then neglect to put that name into your system? Even the most experienced and sophisticated businesses can fall apart when basic marketing organization has been allowed to slip. First, even the most brilliant marketing campaign can collapse if people who inquire do not get a response or if there is no follow-up. (It happens.) Second, the chances are slim that a prospect is ready to buy precisely at the moment of contact. Direct marketers go back for the order at least three times over an 18-month period. A quarterly program of calling and mailing is better. If you organize prospects in your computer, you can contact a few each day. This makes following up a less daunting task than after completing a periodic mass mailing or telephone blitz.

SUREFIRE TIP

An excellent source of "how to" information and reviews of the newest hardware and software suited specifically for the small or home-based business is *Home Office Computing* magazine. Subscription information: 800-288-7812; problems, questions: 800-288-7812; Internet Web site: http://smalloffice.com; on America Online: key words hoc, soho.

Take a good look at the software you've been using. If your system for organizing your marketing is in the range of poor to nonexistent, you have at least three choices on how to manage prospects and stay organized:

1. **Organizer programs.** These inexpensive programs include a daily calendar on which you can post calls to be made, to-do items, an hourly schedule, and a list of long-range tasks. A second feature is a card file for entering data and notes on your prospects, and from which you can print labels. A third feature is an electronic filing cabinet, in which you can create hundreds of individual files under topics of your choosing. Usually organizer programs also have a simple word processing program so you can write letters while sorting through your daily list of tasks.
2. **Contact management programs.** These are similar to organizer programs but more powerful. Contact management programs are most useful for full-time sales and marketing people who work from home and mobile offices instead of conventional office space. Often they have networking capabilities that allow swapping information between the home office and other off-site offices.
3. **Database programs.** These programs are for managing a lot of information and relating important items. For example, a database program can give you information on everybody who responded to the ad coded Dept. XYZ and spent more than $500, but didn't respond until they received the third mailing and haven't been active since.

My computer is set up with both an organizer program and a database program. The organizer program is the first thing to appear on the screen when the computer is turned on, showing me key appointments, calls, and to-dos for the day. Names and addresses stored in the card file are my "active" contacts—people with whom I currently have frequent contact. When current projects end, those names are moved into the database file under the "prospects" category. These are the folks who get calls and mailings from time to time along with other former clients who, hopefully, are between projects with me. Because there is a word processing program that works with the database program, I can print personalized notes and letters and send them only to names I select. (This type of feature is common among the various programs offered by the major software companies.) I avoid using labels for prospect mailings and try to make them as personal as possible, but I do use address labels for postcard mailings.

If you've been diligent about organizing your prospects and marketing, congratulations. It is one of the disciplines people know about—like exercising and improving your diet—but fail to accomplish because the day is filled with more urgent things to do.

If you're starting from scratch, you can design any organizational format that fits your needs, but it will probably look something like this:

List: Prospect
Type: Client (You can create a code that helps you sort past clients from cold calls, etc., or by industry group, year, or whatever would help you sort them.)
Title: Vice President
Greeting: Ms.
First Name: Dawn
Last Name: Smith
Company: Connectivity, Inc.
Address: 13 rue Madelaine
Address 2: P.O. Box 3333
City: Topeka
State/Province: KS
Postal Code: 12345
Phone: xxxxxxxx
Fax: xxxxxxxx
e-mail: xxxxxxxx
Other Contacts: Walter Mitty, President
Goal(s): Assess outlook for new business
Next Step: Call after first of the year . . . new budget time
Next Contact Date: January 12
Comments: Pleased with last project. Seasonal. Contact after first of year for summer projects. Tied up in meetings every Monday. Call Tuesday after 4 PM.

Suppose your first goal is to penetrate the voice mail and set up a meeting.

Enter this in the "goals" field of your database or organizer file. It then becomes a reminder of where you left off, an important aid when you begin to deal with many prospects at varying stages in the selling cycle. Next, place the client's name on your organizer's to-do or to-call file to remind you to follow up. In the example above, you would enter it on January 12, the date in the "Next Contact Date" field. On January 12 it will pop up on your calendar, and you can review the prospect's file to remind yourself about the goals and status. If you don't call, the reminder automatically will be advanced to the next day and the next, gently nagging you until you meet the objective. Here are some tips for your database:

- Make notes in your prospect's record when you identify a pattern that spells success or failure. For example, some prospects work odd hours or split their weeks between a business office and a home office. I like to keep track of their work patterns.
- Many of these software programs have a "find" or search feature that allows you to identify all the records you have tagged for follow-up on January 12. If you use the feature, your daily marketing effort will be organized and simplified.
- Be slow to drop people from the prospect list. I clean my list by removing prospects whose situations have changed—death or bankruptcy are good reasons. When I'm really stuck for new prospects, I go back to the list of former clients that have been dormant for a long time. I'll call them just to catch up on what they're doing. From time to time, I have started doing business again with a client I had assumed was out of the question.
- Whenever you talk to a client on a marketing call, enter a few key words from the conversation in the "Comments" field so you can pick up where you left off ("When I spoke to you in October, you mentioned you would be interested in talking about a new [whatever] now that this year's funds are available . . . .").
- Before you begin your daily follow-up calls, print out each prospect's record so you have the goal clearly in mind. Make notes and update the record immediately after the call with a new goal, follow-up date, and client information.

As I wrote this chapter, my phone rang and provided me with an example of the importance of marketing. It was a friend who owns a bed and breakfast, and he was in a panic because his peak season was approaching and he had no business on the books. We had spoken prior to this call, and he had told me he had "probably a thousand" names and addresses of people who had visited. He told me he had never organized them to do a customer mailing. I had urged him to organize the names and write a letter about the many improvements he had made to his inn, but he had not yet done either. Because he couldn't find the names of the businesses I had given him who could help him get organized (he doesn't use a computer), he wanted to know what to do. "I hate this marketing stuff," he grumbled. He wanted only to work on his building and tend the garden. Realizing the necessity of good marketing to fill the beds, this time he promised to call for help getting organized. I'd be willing to bet, though, that if his phone rings and he books a few rooms today, he'll think the crisis is over, will never get organized, and will call in a worse panic a month from now, wondering again what to do.

Most people "hate this marketing stuff." They start out strong, and with good intentions. Then, a month, a year, or 18 months later the marketing effort has unraveled. The road to hell is paved with good intentions. Don't take that road.

Trolling and Casting

Over the years, by trial and error, I have developed a marketing strategy I call "trolling and casting." Both are fishing terms. Although folks in the corporate world are very fond of sports metaphors such as "teamwork" and "carry the ball," the situation of the solo worker is much more like the lone angler, going one on one with the fish. In trolling, the angler gets into a boat, puts some baited lines into the water, and then slowly motors back and forth over an area that is likely to be a good habitat for fish, hoping something will bite.

The trolling part of the marketing strategy has two simple purposes. One is to cover a lot of territory in search of new prospects in order to be visible and accessible. The tactics here involve getting out to business meetings and functions, accepting every speaking engagement offered, and frequenting places that are good habitats for prospects. The goal is to constantly meet new people and collect their business cards, then get them onto your prospect list if they are at all interested in your services or are in a position to refer someone.

The second trolling tactic is to methodically use publicity to increase your visibility and improve your credibility. (This will be discussed further in Chapter 4.) You can't expect trolling to produce immediate results, so don't stop if miracles don't happen right away. From experience I know that if you stop trolling your world begins to shrink, the prospect list goes dry, and you start to fade from memory. In fact, once in awhile it does produce instant results.

Trolling is also an antidote for work-at-home inertia, that laziness about breaking a comfortable routine that can become a deadly form of reclusiveness. Attending a business event, trade meeting, or conference puts you back in touch with the energy of the business world and gets you out of those sweatpants and slippers with the bunny ears. At one such meeting, I had lunch with a person I had known for 20 years. He said he was about to look for someone to work on a video. I reminded him that I worked in video. We did his project, which led to many more similar projects over the course of several years. He hadn't thought of me before that lunch. Out of sight, out of mind—even with a 20-year history.

Casting is targeting. You know there is a big bass hiding under a lily pad, or a wily trout lurking in a deep hole along the riverbank, and now it is a question of getting the right combination of timing, placement, and bait together to make that fish take action. You also know that a fish will act for its own reasons, not yours. Only rarely do things happen on the first cast. If you worked through evaluating your market, you already have an idea of who and where the prospect is, how palatable your bait is, and something about timing. Casting now becomes the sequence of calling and mailing that will lead to a meeting, a proposal, and, hopefully, business.

Why People Buy

It can be frustrating to see so clearly why someone should buy your services, but will turn you down. A lot of rejection has to do with timing. People don't scratch what doesn't itch, and I have never been able to sell something to someone who wasn't inter-

Putting all your eggs in one basket. In the best of all possible worlds, no one customer or client will represent more than 25 percent of your income. This is a goal worth striving toward and building into your marketing plan.

Ignoring seasonal fluctuations. Several of us work-at-homes were comparing notes one day and hit a common theme of having business drop dead in the summer. If your current projects wrap up in May or June, you'll find yourself marketing into July and August when a lot of people are on vacation and decisions aren't being made. For businesses that budget on a calendar year, by the middle of summer the money is committed. There may be a little left in the cookie jar, but finding someone to spend it in August is difficult. You can be in serious cash flow trouble before things start to get back to normal after Labor Day.

For the same reason, March, April, and May are good times for a marketing push to make sure your factory is full going into the summer.

Losing your self-confidence. There must be people working solo who have never hit a dry spell, but I have never met one. These are periods when you simply can't seem to do anything right and you lose every proposal you write. No one returns your phone calls. Your letters seem to have been lost in the mail. The goldfish nips at you when you feed it. You have an urge to go outside and stand in the sunshine to see if you still cast a shadow; maybe you're dead and just don't know it.

Don't give up. There is only one way to get out of that kind of trouble: Sell your way out. Start by calling those old clients who have been almost written off as prospects for new business. Ask them what's new. You may be calling them at the right time.

Becoming reclusive or distracted. Working from home can be seductive, leading to puttering around or putting hobbies and errands ahead of tending to business. Change the routine. Get back to a 9 to 5 routine, and get dressed up and go to business functions. Join the chamber of commerce. Take a course. Book a lunch or breakfast date with a client or prospect. Whatever the business loop is, stay in it. Put an outside event on your calendar today.

Troubleshooting

Those of us who were self-employed before and during the recession of the early 1990s will not forget it very soon. Friends and business associates became casualties. Nothing worked. The times were simply out of control.

In normal times, however, every business that is having problems can start troubleshooting by looking at the tripod that supports business: product, price, and promotion. Here are some questions to consider in each area:

- *Product.* Are the features and benefits of your product on target and up to date with the competition? Is the market shrinking or too full of competitors? Have people moved on to different products, never to return? Has quality slipped?
- *Price.* Too high? Too low? Has your specialty become a commodity, with competitors undercutting it?
- *Promotion.* Have you been forgotten? Is the mix (advertising, publicity, direct sales, direct mail, etc.) wrong? Do you need another opinion? What do your clients or customers think? Are you distinguishing yourself from competitors by stressing features and benefits?

If one of the legs on the tripod is shorter than the others, your business will become wobbly. Some marketers add "positioning" or "place" as the fourth "p." Positioning is your niche in the marketplace, and how you are viewed relative to your competitors. Place, or location, is a critical consideration not only for retailers, but also for service providers. You don't need to be on an interstate highway intersection, but it helps to be in an area with a healthy economy.

It is very easy to get off track. Working alone, it is easy to be pulled by the demands of the day and the absolute necessity to keep business flowing. Consequently, cumulative daily decisions may lead in directions that are not in the best long-term interest of the business. About four times a year—at the beginning of each quarter—pause and compare the reality of where you are headed with your plans for where you want to be.

In fact, why not start today? Begin by answering these four questions:

1. To get where I want to go, a year from today my three largest customers should be . . .
2. In addition to (or instead of) the services or products I offer today, I should also . . .
3. To make this business really work, I have to learn how to . . .
4. Who can I call today that can help me get where I want to go?

CHAPTER 3

Smart Marketing Tactics Pay Dividends

"I am a great believer in luck, and I find that the harder I work the more I have of it."

—Stephen Leacock

*N*o doubt you've noticed that the solo, self-employed, work-at-home must constantly strive to be taken seriously. Even among people in the corporate world who envy the apparent freedom, there is a nagging doubt about whether or not the home business is really serious. It is all too easy to move out of the stream in which business takes place and be forgotten.

People who leave corporations to fly with the eagles often notice that they are treated differently when they no longer operate under the strength of that corporate logo. The logo conferred a certain amount of power and status. They were more useful with those corporate resources behind them, particularly to people who wanted to sell something.

"Nobody pays any attention to me anymore," lamented a retired man I met in Florida. He had been the president of a very large corporation, but now, without the power of the logo, he was treated just like everyone else in the affluent, behind-the-guarded-gates community.

Because being a home-based business has built-in hurdles, it becomes very important to develop a set of tactics or habits to overcome them. This requires refocusing on the things you can do to make sure your business continues to be:

- Accessible
- Credible
- Visible

Your Secret Weapon Is You—Make the Most of It

Once the initial excitement of starting up your own business has passed, it may be hard to remember that as a lone operator, you are the logo. You are the secret weapon. You may not have the resources and power of Microsoft behind you, but you have a unique advantage: People buy from people they like and trust. Yes, there are exceptions. The race isn't always to the swift or the victory to the strong, but that's the way to bet. And relationships don't always count for everything, but that's also the way to bet. You are the logo. You must respect, honor, and promote the living daylights out of your logo, even if you're getting a little tired of "the marketing stuff." As you enter year two and run the risk of becoming "old news," you can't afford to be modest.

12 Marketing Habits

Without the discipline of an organization and manager riding herd on you, over time there is a risk of trading good habits for bad ones and letting your marketing slip. I've seen it happen to myself and to other home-based workers because of the peculiar nature of working alone in a relaxed setting. I've noted a dozen areas where discipline can get a bit flabby. Is it happening to you? Take the following self-test of your marketing habits.

1. Are you building new face-to-face business relationships? You do not meet prospective clients by hanging around your office. Get out of the house. Find where your potential customers gather—conferences, trade shows, professional societies, chambers of commerce, volunteer and sports organizations, even certain breakfast places are all possibilities. Local newspapers are full of this kind of information. Volunteer organizations are excellent places to meet people on neutral territory and do worthwhile things at the same time.

The hardest time to find new business is when you are not doing any business and are out of the loop. It is amazing how fast you can be forgotten. After a year or two you may find yourself at the center of a small and shrinking universe. Face-to-face meetings are very important. Once the business chemistry is established, the necessity for frequent meetings diminishes.

2. Do you still relentlessly pursue referrals? Did you ever? A very successful financial planner told me nearly all of her business growth was based on referrals from her wealthy clients. It was no accident. She would offer a discount on her services if, after a period of time, the client was satisfied and would write letters to three friends making a modest recommendation. The planner drafted the letters and let her clients modify them.

Using a personal reference has the power to make or break the chances of setting up a meeting and establishing a business relationship. It's the credibility issue; use it whenever you can.

3. Have you learned to practice shameless self-promotion? Build a press list of your local media out of the yellow pages. Add publications you read that cover your business or profession. Send out a release when you start, expand, move, add staff, or win a major account (with client permission, of course). It's a good idea to include selected prospects on your press release mailing list, too.

Invite yourself to be a speaker at seminars and conferences, discussing your area of expertise. Offer to write a story or column for a local newspaper or business publication on some topic of interest to the readership. For more on using publicity, see Chapter 4.

4. Are you constantly expanding your prospect database? A shrinking prospect list could mean the "terrible twos" are around the corner. Keep it current and, as I have suggested, use it frequently.

5. Are you trying to sell by "remote control" instead of selling in person? One reason the Internet is so appealing is that it promises you can talk to millions of people without doing much of anything beyond posting a Web page. You can market by "remote control," or so it seems. Don't bet your business on it. Many sole proprietors have never had to sell one on one; the marketing department worried about those things. That fact alone can be at the heart of the problem if you can't get new business. Here's a quick review of a typical sequence of events in marketing to new prospects:

- Identify a prospect.
- Write down a specific sales or marketing objective. Very often this initial objective is not to "sell," but to "make a meeting" that will allow you to learn more about the client and then frame a proposition that will sell.
- Make a cold telephone call to set up a meeting. If you get voice mail, leave your name and say you will call back. No more.
- Once you've penetrated the voice mail and set up the meeting, confirm the time and purpose in writing. Don't call to confirm—this gives them a chance to reschedule.
- Write down your specific goals for the outcome of the meeting. Yes, the goal certainly is to make the deal or get the sale, but in a first meeting it often is to gather the information that will allow you to come back with a proposal that really resonates for this prospect. Now is the time to frame the "most important questions" that you will want answered at your meeting (discussed in the next step).
- The meeting begins. Outline the reason for the meeting (often it is to explore mutual opportunities in doing business with each other), then listen and ask questions. It may be too soon to try to sell. People buy for their reasons, not yours. Your task is to find out what you can do for them that will trigger that action. Get an overview of their business. Understand their problems and goals.

Marketing Tactics Pay Dividends 33

ortant questions to ask are:
ost important to you when it comes to . . .
ou see the problem . . .

ers can provide the key to finding out how you
ness together because these are the goals or
be addressed.

eeting. Once you understand the priorities, a
me to sum up what you understand the situa-
nd make an offer: "So, if I came to you with a
did x and y and z, would you be interested in
at it?" Or, "May I come back to you with some
on how we could. . . ." Make specific arrange-
next step, which is typically a meeting to lay
osal.

our car or the nearest coffee shop and flesh
s of your notes. If the situation didn't allow for
, do a memory dump and get key points down
sually, it is perfectly fine to take notes during
, but it's a good idea to first ask your prospect
with them.

is to go back to the office and "connect the
a proposal that meets as many of the param-
ee Chapter 5 for help with proposal writing.)
ry job begins with a proposal that covers the
wants to know:

rstand my problem, or what I want to accom-
plish?
- Can you solve my problem? How?
- Why are you better than the three other people I'm inter-
viewing?
- How much will it cost?

The objective for the second meeting is to present the proposal and make the deal. Jack Falvey, president of INTERMARK of
Londonderry, New Hampshire, is one of the country's most successful sales consultants. He suggests preparing for cold telephone calls and important meetings by taking a 3 × 5 card and
dividing it into thirds (see Figure 3.1). The top one-third is a written objective for the outcome of the call or meeting. The middle

FIGURE 3.1 Preparing a Card Like This Can Help You Make the Most of Your Meeting with a Prospect

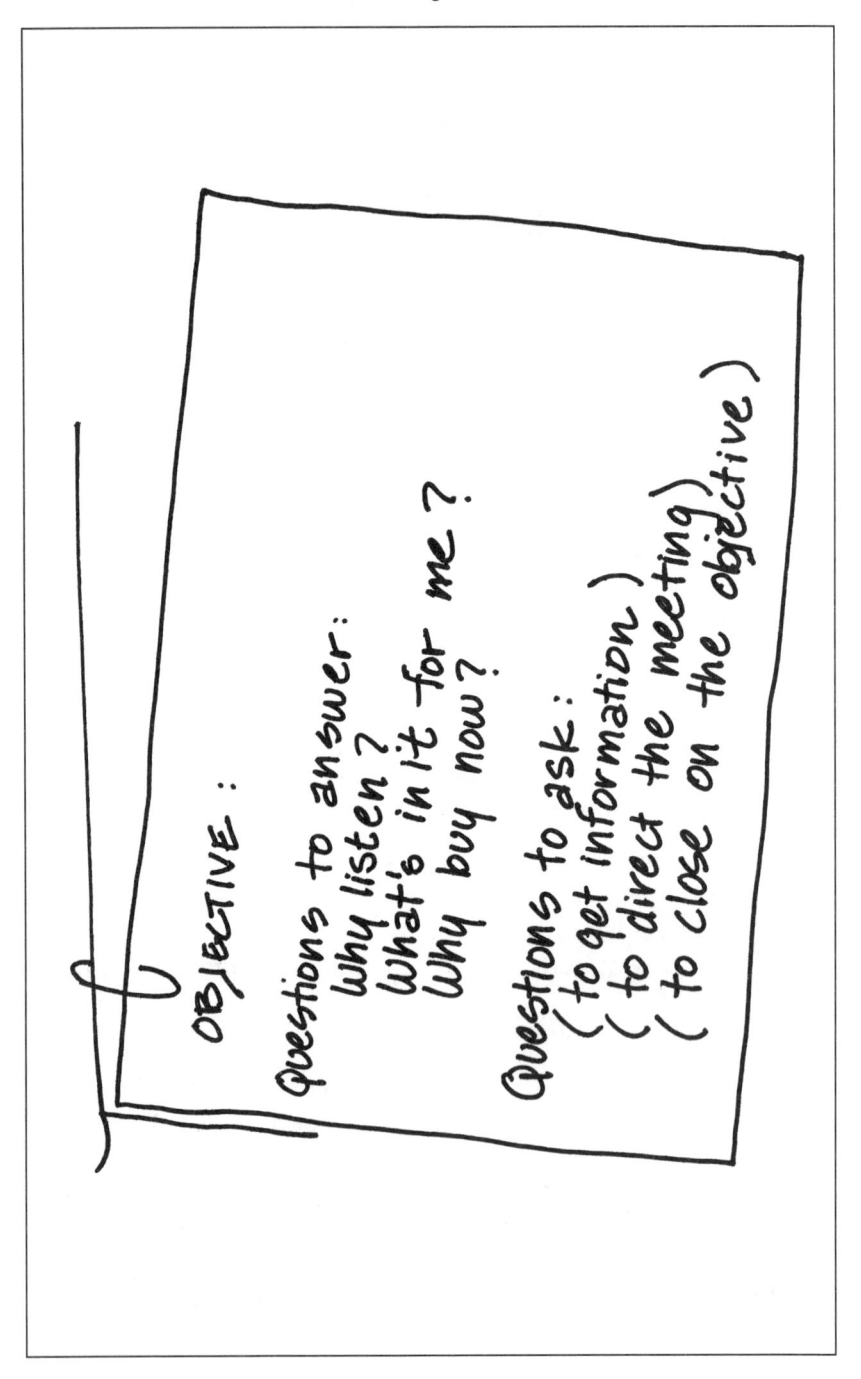

OBJECTIVE :

Questions to answer:
Why listen?
What's in it for me?
Why buy now?

Questions to ask:
(to get information)
(to direct the meeting)
(to close on the objective)

third is a reminder that you must be ready to answer your prospect's three major questions:

1. Why should I listen to you?
2. What's in this for me?
3. Why should I act or buy now?

The bottom third of the card contains questions that do three things: gather information, take the meeting in the direction of your goal, and lead to a closing (e.g., "May I come back with a proposal that . . .") Clip the card to your note pad or pocket calendar so you can easily refer to it during the meeting or call. Nobody will ask you, "What is that?" The most successful salespeople write down their goals, and they are good listeners.

It's up to you to control the transaction, and that means preparing in advance for how you will respond to all the possible objections that can be raised. This requires skills that are developed only through practice.

SUREFIRE TIP

In client relations: listen, learn, and lead. We've talked about listening and learning. Leading your client is a matter of using your knowledge and expertise to arrive at solutions or action plans your client may not know about or hasn't considered. Clients do not want to tell you what to do, they want you to tell them what to do. *That is why you are there.*

---

6. Have you thought about how you look to your customers? It is very easy to give credence to the assumption that people who work at home aren't seriously in business. In the rush and expense of getting started you may have taken some shortcuts that you intended to fix later, but by now you've gotten used to them or don't want to spend the money. Ask yourself:

- Do my business card and letterhead look professional or do they look like they were turned out on a PC with a business card template? Maybe you need a graphic designer to help you create a new look.

- Am I in the yellow pages, the business pages of the phone book, and listed in the appropriate business directories?
- When people call, does it sound like a business is answering? While working on a project recently, I was interested in buying a mailing list of work-at-homes. A list broker claimed to have one, so I asked how they got the names. The answer: "We do a lot of telephone surveys of businesses. When we get someone with a baby crying in the background we put them down as a work-at-home." Is that your business image? A home business telephone system can and should be as businesslike as those found in large companies. Get a business line—you may even be able to deduct it from your taxes.
- How do I look? You may sit around and work at your computer in a sweat suit and fuzzy slippers with bunny ears, but that's not the way to look on the street during business hours. Working from home is not an excuse to look like a bum. Your potential clients may assume you are unemployed, retired, or living on a trust fund. The issue is not one of wearing a white shirt and tie. It is a question of what is appropriate for your kind of business and the customers or clients you see. When in doubt, dress like your customers, because they will feel comfortable.

7. Do you constantly refine your "Unique Selling Proposition"? The USP is an advertising concept. It is the "so what?" of what you do or sell. You build it into your marketing plan. Whatever it is today, strive to make it better by constantly testing new ideas on people you meet. Watch closely for their reaction. Do they "get it"? Practice describing what you do in terms that show how you solve problems or satisfy what your clients want. Be specific. Would you hire someone who claimed to do everything from management consulting to short order cooking and desktop publishing?

One day, several of us marketing types were talking about an acquaintance who had been testing USPs in the personal columns of the newspaper. After several attempts, the winning headline proposition was "love hugs." It produced the most inquiries, led to some interesting breakfast meetings, and was responsible for a romantic trip to Europe. (Naturally, the copywriters in our marketing group tried to come up with something that would beat it. Although it has yet to be tested, the winning proposition was "Learn French, kissing.")

8. Are you a good listener? The best salespeople are good listeners. They are anxious to hear the answers to the questions mentioned earlier: "What's most important to you?" and "How would you describe the problem?" One common listening problem is tuning someone out while you develop your response to something they have said. Instead, see if you can rephrase what they have just said in a way that advances your goal (coming back with a proposal, for example).

9. Are you following up on leads? Follow-up is where most of us fail so it is important to develop a system. Mine involves a pocket Day Runner, a computer organizer program, and a desktop book divided into days of the month for handling pieces of paper. Most important is setting aside five or ten minutes at the end of the day to organize priorities and your followups for the next day.

10. Are you marketing hard when you are busiest? By now you have discovered that work loads for work-at-homes are often waves and troughs, with the consequences being an irregular cash flow. It's a lesson I learn over and over: One day you can be overwhelmed and a few days later a project or product is delivered and there is nothing new to do. Then, because of the lead time most projects take to develop, you are stuck in the dead zone for too long. The result is fear, and the fear is justified. Thus, it is important to continue to market during these busy times so that you can find new work to help fill your next down period.

11. Do you hand out too much information? When you're anxious to sell it is a natural tendency to overwhelm people with information. Don't show too much, talk too much, or send too much stuff through the mail. You run the risk of being ignored or presenting something that will turn off clients. I prefer one-page personal letters, personal note cards, or even postcards for written communication. Invite requests for more information; try to set up a meeting to provide it. This is a way to keep the dialogue going, while burying people in materials can end it. So, when in doubt, avoid bounding out in front of your prospect showing everything you can muster.

12. Are you using the most effective marketing arrow? I like to think of the various marketing techniques as a quiver full of different arrows, each with a distinct set of strengths and weaknesses. Marketing arrows work best when they are used in combination. They do not all have to be used together. Marketing arrows are things like:

- Advertising
- Collateral materials like brochures, sell sheets, and so on
- Direct mail
- Direct sales
- Internet
- Partnering or "work-linking"
- Publicity and public relations
- Telephone marketing
- Events like workshops and seminars

We've discussed the steps in direct selling, and we'll cover publicity in Chapter 4. Now let's take a look at some of the other options.

A Closer Look at Marketing "Arrows"

Advertising

When people first go into business for themselves they are often tempted to buy advertising because it seems to be what real businesses do. If you have tried advertising and it hasn't worked, don't be surprised or disappointed. Some advertising produces nothing but calls from more people selling advertising. It is hard for a solo operator to be able to afford to make a real impact with advertising. You can think of advertising as an attempt to get "shelf space" in the minds of prospective clients. As a small operator, you are a six-pack of a generic soft drink. You don't have enough money to position yourself against Coke or Pepsi or even Dr. Pepper through advertising. But if you are visible (on the shelf of the supermarket of the mind) somebody will buy you . . . particularly if you are at hand when someone is thirsty. Timing is everything.

Businesses—even home-based businesses—vary so widely that it is difficult to make a blanket statement about what works, but here are three rules of thumb.

First, budget for repetition and continuity instead of a one-time, big-space blowout. Try listings, business directories, and public radio. Second, put your USP to work in your advertising copy. This is one of the reasons to spend time refining it. Finally, use advertising at the same time as other marketing arrows for repetition and impact. Don't count on advertising alone to keep your factory full.

Collateral Materials—Letterhead, Brochures, and Such

After a year or two, it's time to reexamine your marketing materials to ensure they still pack a punch. Are your prospects seeing the same old thing over and over again? Computers have made desktop marketing a rapidly changing and competitive field. Imagine you are getting your own marketing package in the mail. Is it creative and tempting or boring and predictable? After a couple of years, it's probably time for a change.

Clever as you may be with a computer, I'd suggest you take your existing material to a graphic designer and create a fresh look to support your push for new business. Make sure your USP is as strong as you can make it and that it is the cornerstone of your material. Give your designer clearly defined goals and constraints (like cost) and samples of materials you like.

A typical marketing package includes a scope of services or product description, which describes precisely what you do or sell, a statement of your experience, credentials, or qualifications, and a list of past and current clients. Custom pieces can be slipped in with a general package to focus on the items specifically appropriate to a prospect's interests or situation.

Sending out a newsletter also can be a good way to keep your name in front of your prospects as long as it meets three criteria: it is visually interesting, short and to the point, and genuinely useful to your prospects. Useful information can be "how to" articles on your field of expertise, or news or industry trends that have an impact on your prospects. People have too much reading material already, so it is essential that a newsletter doesn't just talk about you, but performs a service.

Direct Mail

If you already tried direct mail, you have learned how tricky it can be. It is an easy way to spend a lot of money with meager results. For mass mailings, a response rate of 2 or 3 percent is considered good. Targeted mailings to your prospect list are part of the "casting" strategy. The criteria here are: short, personal, to the point, and followed up with a call. Postcards fall into the "We are pleased to announce . . ." category, which can include awards won, accomplishments, and news. They also are useful for confirming a meeting date or for brief "thanks" messages.

Postcards are inexpensive to imprint with your logo and return address. Artists, designers, photographers, or struggling actors should invest in postcards with full-color artwork or photos on one side. An announcement for a gallery exhibition would be a good example. People who provide high-technology services have had good response by buying mailing lists of attendees at conferences in their specialty and sending postcards inviting inquiries for an information package. These are followed up with a call that leads to a meeting.

SUREFIRE TIP

Photographers frequently send full-color samples of their work to their client list as a reminder. A photographer friend suggests Modern Postcard of Carlsbad, California. They can provide quality, four-color reproduction on one side of a standard 4 × 6 postcard and brief text on the other for under $100 for 500 postcards. 800-959-8365. Other sizes and formats are available.

Personal letters and notecards are very effective in reconnecting with prospects on a regular basis. We use them interchangeably and follow up with a telephone call. A new person joining you, for example, would warrant a personal letter and a press release. Once your prospect list is organized, sending out a few letters or notecards a day becomes routine. Try also to do a quarterly mailing to all prospects on a slowly rotating basis.

These letters are never more than one page long, and should not look anything like a mass mailing. Follow up with a phone call. This often leads to a valuable update on a prospect's business and a chance to look for an opportunity to do business. It may take months to pay off, but it is worth the effort. I've had competitors move in on my "dormant" clients simply by hitting them at the right time, and you never know when that will be unless you make it a point to stay in contact.

The Internet

If you are not already on the Internet, you are probably wondering if the century's biggest parade is passing you by. The Internet is the current miracle diet pill of marketing. Marketing and dieting have a lot in common: Everyone is searching for the silver bullet, the magic potion that will take the work out of it. But the Internet is not the magic potion for everyone.

The top-selling items on the Internet are computer-related gear, travel packages, and pornography. More than 25,000 new Web sites are activated each month. The Internet is becoming a flea market the size of Texas.

If you love the idea of marketing on the Internet, conduct an experiment. Imagine you are trying to find yourself on the Internet. Launch a key word search by region or by product classification. Who is out there like you? Send them an e-mail and ask them specifically if they would recommend the Internet. People talk a lot about "hits" on their Web site, but the real question is whether or not this translates into real business.

The haunting question remains: Who is making money on Internet marketing? Only about one out of five of the magazine publishers on the Net has turned a profit through subscription sales. Many Web sites look dated and forgotten by their Webmasters. But it works for some people. We have business associates who launched a teleconferencing business, put it on the Web, and connected with a huge international electronics manufacturer with an interest in worldwide teleconferencing. That hit made their business, which has since merged with another larger business.

So, results are spotty and it seems to take a long time for most investments in the Internet to pay off. Considering that a Web site has to be hot-linked to other sites to be effective, that it must be updated frequently, and that both good leads and bad leads must be sorted out, the question is: Is the Internet the best place to spend your time and money? Not if you only market locally and the Internet is the only thing you are going to use.

Partnering or "Work-Linking"

Are you involved in "partnering" with other small operators? Partnering, which also can be called "work-linking," virtual companies, strategic alliances, networks, consortiums, collaboratives, and teams, is a good way to grow your business without expanding your space or getting into the complexities of hiring employees. It expands your universe by allowing you to team up with other small or home-based businesses to take on big projects you couldn't tackle alone, and by having more people at work marketing partnered services. Partnering can create some strange bedfellows, and sometimes that is a positive when it looks like a negative. Usually, the catalyst for partnering is a request for proposal that includes components very small businesses cannot handle alone.

There are two steps to partnering: Identify a partner who has the necessary skills and with whom you can work in comfort, and divide up the work. Keeping an eye out for potential business partners is a good reason for going to business functions. Check around to see if they have a solid reputation, and whether their prices are reasonable. Normally, there is a "lead" partner, under whose name the job is done, and an associated partner (or partners), who is identified as the principal subcontractor. Egos do play a role when someone is new in the business world and partnering for the first time, but for experienced businesses it becomes routine. I partnered on the very first projects I took on when the business was first established, and more than half of the company's current projects involve at least one other partner.

If there is an existing request for proposal with a work description, it's fairly easy to divide the responsibilities by putting initials next to each "task" sentence or paragraph, and reaching an agreement on who does which task. If there is no request for proposal, you should get together to define the parameters of the work, write individual proposals, and then incorporate them into a final, single document. The lead business gets to compile the proposal, but it must have everyone's agreement.

Partnering requires a level of trust, but its benefits outweigh its disadvantages. It expands your marketing force, because your partner may run into things you don't hear about. It also helps to overcome one of the curses of working alone: not having anyone available for bouncing ideas around.

Telephone Marketing

Do you avoid making "cold" marketing calls because you find them horribly painful and can't stand rejection? Join the club. Few people enjoy cold calling, but it is an essential part of the marketing mix. Many techniques are taught, but my feeling is that if you don't find a way of calling that suits your personality, you will find a way to avoid it unless you have someone standing over you cracking a whip. I look forward to the day when I will no longer have to do any "smiling and dialing," but I fear it will never come.

The most effective approach I've found is quite simple and based on the listen, learn, lead sequence. The call should be preceded by a letter introducing your services and timed to coincide with when that letter arrives on your prospect's desk. (This, by the way, is why you need to organize your marketing.) Don't ask if they received the letter, assume they did or they soon will. If you get voice mail, simply leave your name and say you will call again. Sometimes this becomes a game of who wears down first. But once connected, the sequence typically unfolds like this:

1. Identify yourself and your business. If you have been referred by someone and can use their name, do it now. Ask if this is a good time to call, in order to determine if they are in the middle of a meeting.
2. Explain how you got their name and why you're calling. Never do random calls—the names should come from trolling or by keeping an eye out for prospects. So explain that you saw a story in the newspaper, or noticed that you attended the same conference, or whatever the case may be: ". . . and I was wondering if you use (your service or product) or have considered trying it?"
3. Listen carefully for a problem you can solve. Deal with objections right away without being argumentative—citing the success of someone in a similar business is a good approach.
4. Talk about benefits: "Our clients have found that by using our services they. . . ."
5. Make an offer (or decide not to): "If I could put together a proposal that would (solve a problem), would you consider it?" Find out when you could get together to learn more about their business.

Strive to make these calls a conversation between two professional people who could have a reason to do business together. Stay away from a scripted hard sell, but structure the conversation to lead in the right direction. Some people will never be clients, and you have to accept that, but it also may be the start of a business relationship that won't blossom for a year or more. Timing is important. Don't believe "no" is the answer until you've heard it three times.

If the prospect doesn't use your service and probably could benefit from doing so, send along a generic marketing piece on the benefits of your service. These brochures are often available from trade groups or associations you may belong to. If not, use a news article. If, at the end of 18 months, the answer is still no, move on.

Seminars and Special Events

If you have a consulting or service business, think about plugging into a seminar or workshop as a means of developing new business. One of the people I shared office space with when I was getting started was a financial planner, and recently while conducting our annual review he said he will probably never have to worry about marketing again. Three or four times a year he conducts a seminar on financial planning, organized through the continuing education department of a local college. It keeps a stream of new business coming to his door.

The seminar is a franchised product based on a carefully developed formula: "If you follow the formula, it works just like they told us it would. If you tinker with it, all bets are off."

The sessions are marketed through direct mail pieces—35,000 sent to lists in a 30-mile area. The seminar was, and is, fairly expensive to operate, but it also is one of the marketing silver bullets. The mailers never change except for the dates, they go to the same list over and over again, and they always draw an audience. The seminar is purely informative and does not sell my friend's services, but a self-evaluation sheet is filled out at the end. A predictable number of people will call my friend, bring in the sheets he helped them develop, and become his customers.

He is not the only person who has discovered the power of the workshop or seminar. Not all ventures lend themselves to these events, but topics like buying a home, investing, bargain travel, the Internet, innovative uses of computers, and many other topics are packaged into seminars or workshops. I have developed a two-hour presentation on the fundamentals of public relations and I'm not at all shy about inviting myself to be a speaker. I'm still working with a company that had a representative at one of my presentations four years ago.

To get the ball rolling, create a one-page outline of what you would cover. Then speak to the continuing education department at the local college or university, or approach business groups like the chamber of commerce. The goal is to partner with an organization that can help with the logistics and promotion. In the case of my financial planner, he pays for printing and mailing, while the college provides the facilities and keeps a small enrollment fee, and the seminar still produces enough business to make it worthwhile. Partnering with a college or business organization also conveys the idea that the session is not simply a self-serving promotion event. You must honor that.

Events are also legitimate topics for press releases and will build your credibility as an expert in the field. Possibly you can parlay that into being a columnist or contributor to a business publication in your area. You'll find that you've become accessible, credible, and visible.

Marketing in "Flights"

Have you ever had an annual advertising budget? Or do you wait to be worn down by a media salesperson? To make the most of the money you do spend, try building advertising expenditures into your marketing calendar and coordinating with other efforts like publicity or direct mail. Experienced advertisers often design programs around advertising "flights," a media buy combined with the other "arrows" that last several weeks. For example, seasonal products such as lawn and garden items are marketed by flights of advertising during the peak of the season. Some businesses advertise in flights two or three times a year to keep from being forgotten. Approaching your marketing in coordinated flights is not a substitute for the day in, day out work, but it can provide both a boost for your business and a wonderful experiment in finding a combination that works for you—the silver bullet.

How much should you spend? Established businesses typically spend 3 percent of their annual gross income on advertising. New business or product introductions push that to 12 percent of anticipated gross. Major feature films can have an advertising and promotion budget equal to the production costs of many millions of dollars.

For the solo work-at-home, part of the budget can be a commitment to spend enough time to do a thorough job. It pays to keep trying new things, and when something works roll it out. Lyman Wood, a famous direct marketer, once told a group of us who worked for him: "Keep trying 'til you find what works. Then move the decimal point in your budget a few places to the right."

CHAPTER 4

Public Relations
Stealth Marketing

*"He or she bloweth not their own horn,
the same shall not be blown."*

—David Schaefer

     By the time you've been in business for a couple of years you may have had the good fortune to discover the magic of publicity, the stealth bomber of marketing. Many of my clients come to me after having had a boost in business when, quite by accident, a story about them appeared in the media. Having the media discover you and write a nice story is a piece of good luck, like a bluebird nesting in your yard. These "bluebird" clients decide they want that kind of good luck on a regular basis.

    It is not magic. Half of what you see on the television news or read in the newspapers gets on the air or into print because of someone's skill in public relations. If you haven't tried it, you're missing one of the least expensive and most credible of the "marketing arrows." Once you've had a little luck with publicity and public relations, you'll develop an appetite for this kind of stealth marketing. Ever wonder why some people are in the paper all the time, and some are not? Here are the secrets.

The basic premise is quite simple: Reporters and feature writers do not make news, nor do they have some mysterious gift for sensing where news is taking place. Reporters work hard to find news by attending government meetings, monitoring police radios, calling experts or public figures, checking public records, going to press conferences, listening to the grapevine, and developing local stories about national trends and events, among other means.

People skilled in public relations help journalists by presenting them with ideas that have some kind of news "hook" or angle. What's news? Here are a few ideas:

- Events
- Names
- New products or businesses
- Trends (think of the Internet coverage over the past few years)
- Change, in everything from personnel to business performance
- Helpful information
- Expanding a business, moving it, taking on an impressive new client, introducing a new product, performing a community service, being named to a position in a professional or community organization, making a speech to a group, offering helpful solutions from your field of expertise, and more

It is especially important to focus on public relations after you've been around for a couple of years because by then you are becoming "old news" and your image needs freshening up.

Here's the Trick

Success in publicity is based on your ability to find the news hook. What would be the headline on your story? Can you summarize the news content in three typewritten lines? What's the "so what" of this story? It does not have to be earthshaking news, but the kernel of news should be presented first and succinctly. Are you the first? Newest? Only?

Reporters are not interested in giving your business free advertising, so your ability to get to the point of the story is essential. On the other hand, some people are embarrassed to promote themselves. Don't be. If a reporter or editor picks up your story and runs it, it's because it has a place as news. If they don't run it, don't give up. Keep trying. They might toss the first nine into the wastebasket, but run number ten. You simply may have been overshadowed by other, bigger events of the day.

Why Bother?

Publicity brings in business. Public relations and publicity are both inexpensive and credible. Remember accessibility, credibility, and visibility? News coverage boosts the second two.

Everyone can spot an ad for what it is: Someone saying wonderful things about themselves or their product, and paying big money to do it. News is different. Someone else is saying things about you. Hopefully, they are good things. That's why it is stealth marketing.

If you have any doubts, watch one of the morning network television talk shows and ask yourself: Why is this guest here? Who set it up? What are they promoting? Chances are, a product, event, or a cause is behind it. And a PR person. The exceptions are fast-breaking news stories like disasters, and even then PR people are managing the flow of information.

Successful publicity can be your least expensive, most effective form of promotion. Don't be ashamed to send clippings about your business to prospective clients.

Who Am I?

As a freelance professional, you are an expert in your field. A reporter can quote you as an authoritative source, or as a provider of useful information. Reporters have pet sources—people they trust to quote when writing about certain topics. Usually, it is great to be one of them. So get to know the reporters who cover your field.

You may be other things as well. Decide what they are. Think in terms of "How will I be described between the commas?" For example, notice the words between the commas in this "event" press release:

> Adventure travel agent Sally Carruthers, author of "Down the Esophagus with Gun and Camera," will present a slide show of her recent trip down the Alimentary Canal at 6 PM Thursday at Toad Hall.

or,

> , a consultant on computer networking and president of Nets to You, . . .

Here is an actual one from the business section of our daily newspaper. It has run several times in stories in which we have been quoted about micro business:

> Schaefer, along with two partners, runs MarketReach, Inc., a firm that offers market and public opinion research and other communications services. The firm's three principals work from their homes in separate Vermont towns.

Frequent publicity keeps your name in front of the public, lets people know you have a lot going on in your business, and gives you an aura of being "newsworthy."

Tools and Techniques of the PR Trade

Your Press List

If you have a press list and haven't used it for a while, it probably is out of date, and now is the time to update and expand it. Updating is a fairly simple task, and one that is best done on a continuing basis by keeping an eye on changes in the media. If you don't have a press list, your telephone book's yellow pages will identify the newspapers, television and radio stations, and magazines in your area. Call your local newspaper and ask if they have an information package for people interested in submitting press releases, or at least a directory of reporters and their areas of responsibility. Watch for reporter's bylines to find out who covers stories about your kind of business. Watch the editorial pages for staff directories. I read the morning paper with a coffee cup in one hand and a scissors in the other, clipping information about clients, potential prospects, and changes in the newspaper staff. These go into my "prospect" and "press" lists. The prospects may become one or two of the day's marketing events. The press lists are updated about every two weeks. It is much, much easier to do this on a continuing basis then to try to play catch-up when you're ready to put out a release. Reporters and their responsibilities change constantly.

Build your press list into your database or organizer program so you can sort it, update it, and print labels. It is best, but not always possible, to establish contact with a specific reporter, editor, or news director (for broadcast media) and put their names on your press list. Without these specific names, use "News Director" for radio stations, "Assignment Editor" for television news, and "Business (or whatever is appropriate) Editor" for print publications. Figure 4.1 shows what a typical listing in my database looks like.

Make sure to include fax numbers because press releases with a critical time angle are often faxed to newsrooms. Not all media like to get things by fax, particularly routine stories that could be mailed. Don't overuse the fax. I fax only fast-breaking stories, and then only after talking it over with the reporter. Increasingly, reporters are inviting press release submissions by e-mail, so either note this in the "comments" section or create a new data field for e-mail addresses.

In addition to the local media, be sure you include local, regional, or state business magazines. Work-at-homes are still something of a curiosity, and if reporters know you are out there you may get a call to comment on some aspect of working from home or on your area of expertise.

Finally, there is probably at least one (and possibly many) trade magazine that covers your area of business and/or is read by your clients. Trade magazines are those published for specific interests or areas of business, and rarely show up on newsstands. They are magazines like *Advertising Age, Water Well Journal,* the

FIGURE 4.1 Sample Press Database Entry

List: Press

Type: Business

First name: Financial Desk

Last name:

Company: Reuters America Inc.

Address: 1700 Broadway 31st Floor

Address 2:

City: New York

State/Province: NY

Postal code: 10019

Phone: 212-603-3300

FAX: 212-603-3446

e-mail:

Other contact:

Letter sent:

Follow-up:

Home phone:

Follow-up:

Comments:

Journal of Invasive Cardiology, Dixie Contractor, and *Drovers Journal.* If you subscribe to one, it is easy to look at the front and pick out an editor to put on your press list.

Those of us who work in publicity and public relations subscribe to annual directories that give us the kind of information we need: names of editors who handle specific topics and their telephone numbers, and groupings of magazines by subject area. If you know someone in a PR firm or advertising agency, ask if you can look at their directories or get last year's copy. Typically, these are several volumes and list every daily and weekly newspaper, television and radio station, and magazine in the country. Each volume can cost from $100 to $300. Some of the most popular are:

- Bacon's Directories, from Bacon's Information Inc. 800-753-6675
- *Working Press of the Nation,* 800-521-8110
- *Editor and Publisher Yearbook* (US and International Newspapers) 212-675-4380 (This one could be in your local library reference department.)

I have several Bacon's, which cost $275 per directory. The company also offers press lists on CD-ROM, printed labels sorted in just about any way you want them, and a clipping service.

Maintaining an up-to-date press list in your computer will make the difference between whether you actually have a press relations program or whether you simply keep intending to have one. The truth is, with a little practice, writing a press release takes practically no time at all. The hassle is in getting it out, which is why a lot of press releases die as good intentions.

Crafting the Press Release

A basic one- or two-page press release is appropriate to send out when you hire someone, announce a new service or product, or move. Even as an established business, you make news all the time as you acquire new, high-profile clients (get their permission, of course, and show them a draft of the press release for approval). For my company, the most common press releases are about new clients, the availability of a new video, or the results of surveys that are of general interest. We also watch national trends in our specialty to see if we can provide reporters with a local angle on a national story. The Internet is a topic that has produced countless "local angle" stories.

Many business people hesitate to prepare releases or get to know reporters. They think reporters don't understand or are opposed to businesspeople. Sometimes, during layoffs or downsizing, for example, their past dealing with reporters have been adversarial. In the long run, though, you have a lot more to gain than to lose when you establish good relations with the press. Even if you find yourself in a tough situation that is going to make news you don't want to see in print, you will be better off if you have "banked" some credibility with the press. You may get the benefit of the doubt, instead of just the doubt.

There are only two rules to writing a press release:

1. The news should be in the first paragraph, called the lead.
2. The lead should be no longer than three typewritten lines.

New press release writers tend to bury the lead. After you've written a press release, try throwing away the first paragraph and see if the lead is really in the second. Often it is. The lead tells the story, and the rest of the press release simply elaborates details. Your release should briefly restate who you are and what you do.

Double-space press releases. Keep them short and to the point. Use short sentences. Use short paragraphs. Identify all photos and artwork by writing on the back (a label is better) or attaching a photo caption. Avoid jargon and acronyms.

A sample press release is shown in Figure 4.2. It was sent as an April Fools' Day joke to a few business publications. One statewide publication ran it without comment. Another used it as an example of how to write a press release and continues to hand it out at trade shows. The local chamber of commerce uses it as a handout to instruct new businesses on the basics of press relations. I don't know if it brought in any business, but I got phone calls from complete strangers and heard reports of it being posted on bulletin boards at the university and state government offices. People still ask for copies.

4 / Public Relations 55

FIGURE 4.2 Employee of the Year Press Release

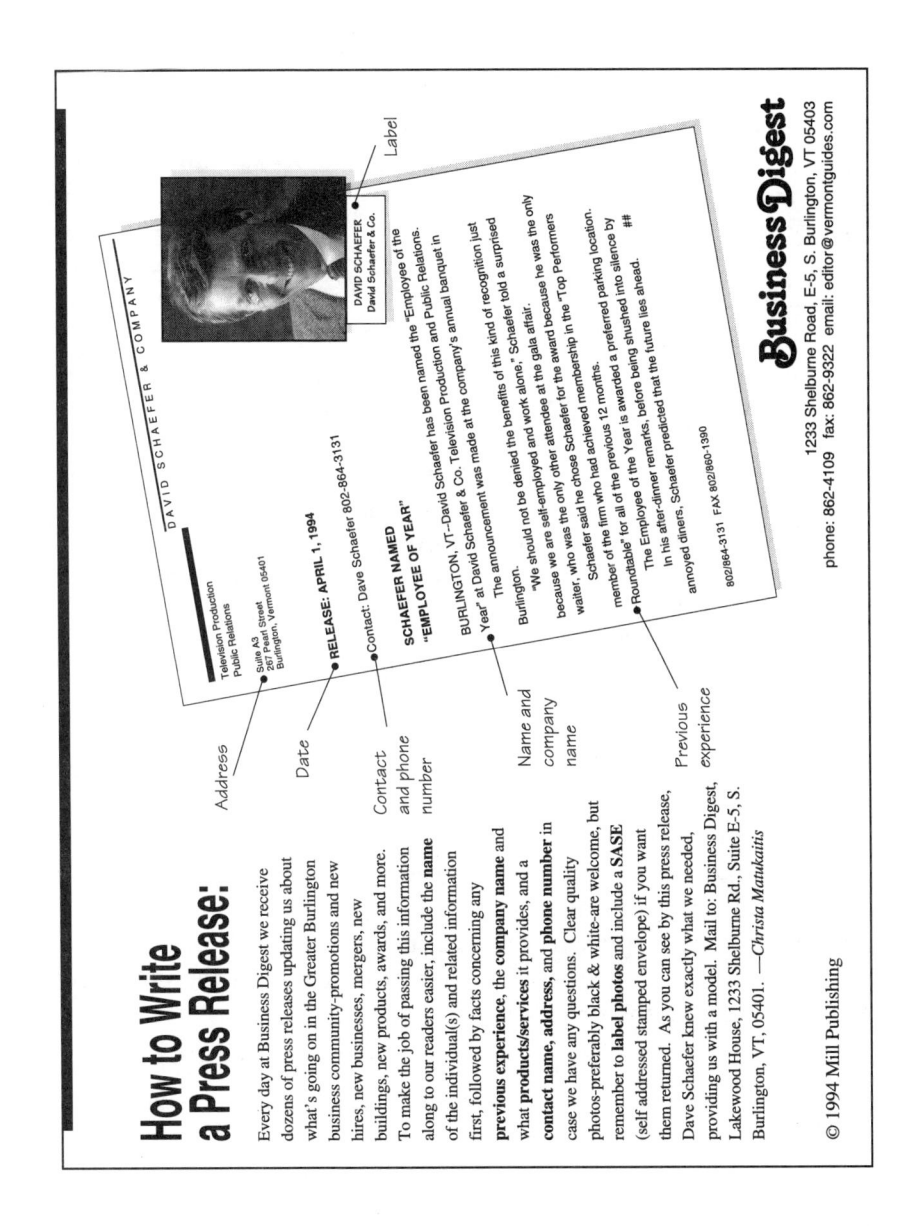

Address

Date

Contact and phone number

Name and company name

Previous experience

Label

DAVID SCHAEFER & COMPANY

Television Production
Public Relations

Suite A3
261 Pearl Street
Burlington, Vermont 05401

RELEASE: APRIL 1, 1994

Contact: Dave Schaefer: 802-864-3131

**SCHAEFER NAMED
"EMPLOYEE OF YEAR"**

BURLINGTON, VT–David Schaefer has been named the "Employee of the Year" at David Schaefer & Co. Television Production and Public Relations.

The announcement was made at the company's annual banquet in Burlington.

"We should not be denied the benefits of this kind of recognition just because we are self-employed and work alone," Schaefer told a surprised and only other attendee at the gala affair.

Schaefer said he chose Schaefer for the award because he was the only waiter, who was the only other attendee at the "Top Performers Roundtable" for all of the previous 12 months. Schaefer is awarded a preferred parking location.

The Employee of the Year is awarded a preferred parking location.

In his after-dinner remarks, before being shushed into silence by annoyed diners, Schaefer predicted that the future lies ahead.   ##

802/864-3131 FAX 802/860-1390

DAVID SCHAEFER
David Schaefer & Co.

Business Digest

1233 Shelburne Road, E-5, S. Burlington, VT 05403
phone: 862-4109   fax: 862-9322   email: editor@vermontguides.com

How to Write a Press Release:

Every day at Business Digest we receive dozens of press releases updating us about what's going on in the Greater Burlington business community–promotions and new hires, new businesses, mergers, new buildings, new products, awards, and more. To make the job of passing this information along to our readers easier, include the **name of the individual(s)** and related information first, followed by facts concerning any **previous experience**, the **company name** and what **products/services** it provides, and a **contact name, address, and phone number** in case we have any questions. Clear quality photos–preferably black & white–are welcome, but remember to **label photos** and include a **SASE** (self addressed stamped envelope) if you want them returned. As you can see by this press release, Dave Schaefer knew exactly what we needed, providing us with a model. Mail to: Business Digest, Lakewood House, 1233 Shelburne Rd., Suite E-5, S. Burlington, VT, 05401. —*Christa Matukaitis*

© 1994 Mill Publishing

What Is in a Press Kit?

If you are about to make your first approach to the press, or if you have a particularly good story to release, I'd suggest putting together a press kit. A press kit is a two-pocket folder that contains a news release plus a package of supporting background material that can include photographs, drawings, and charts. If it is your first press effort, take the opportunity to introduce your business to the press by including background from your marketing materials, such as your scope of service, client list, and basic biographical information. Some of this information will land in the reporters' files, and you may be called months later as an "expert source" on a totally different story that is being developed.

Press kits are often used for new product or new service announcements. Look for opportunities to partner with your client on a newsworthy situation that benefits both of you. These opportunities often come at the end of a project. The "product" may be new information about a subject. A typical new product press kit includes the following:

- Basic press release announcing the product, with a few details; two pages.
- High-quality 8" × 10" color photograph of the product, or, in the case of a service, a photo of you. For portraits, color usually isn't necessary and a smaller black and white is fine.
- Brief examples of how to use the product; one page.
- Biographical sketch of the individual who developed the product; one page.
- Details and specifications of the product; one page.
- Background, history, and "success story" of the company producing the product; two pages.

In this example, some 324 editors and broadcasters got the press kit. Some of the press lists came from my own database; others were purchased. The basic release included a note to editors that said they could get a sample of the product by calling or faxing. About 30 eventually did receive a product and wrote extensively about it. Another 25 editors of large national publications and producers of television talk shows got a product with the press kit. The story ran in newspapers across the country and the product developer was interviewed on CNN. Production was increased and the product was being introduced in France.

The folder is the most expensive part of the press kit. Big companies often produce a jazzy folder just for the product announcement. Small ones buy stock folders and put their mailing label on them, or have a sticker printed for the press kit and other marketing uses.

The next most expensive item is the photo. When having photography done, make it clear to the photographer that you want all rights to the negatives because you plan a mass photo duplication. Custom photo printing is prohibitively expensive for press releases, so go to a mass duplicator that offers a wide range of photo and transparency services, including digital imaging.

The rest of the press kit is basically paper.

A press kit, in the envelope and with postage paid, will cost about $5 each for materials in quantities over 100. This does not include the cost of hiring a photographer, or your time. Good photographs help to sell the story, so don't send snapshot quality photography.

Step by step, developing a press kit looks like this:

1. Write the copy for the pieces and parts of the press kit.
2. Arrange for product photography and artwork.
3. Identify the media and develop the following lists:
    - A small "AA" list that will get the press kit and product (the product could be a book, a new piece of software, etc.). These are the most influential media. Some may reach millions of people, but others may reach a small audience of perfect prospects for your business.
    - A larger "A" list of fairly important media who will not get a sample product.
    - Everybody else on the list. These media cover the subject area of your press kit, but have small circulations.
4. Call everyone on the AA and A lists to make sure there have been no changes to the staff. "I have a press kit on a new product and I want to direct it to the proper person. Are you still handling new products . . .?"
5. The kit goes into the mail.
6. Follow up with calls. Did the kit arrive? Some sample products vanish. What did you think of it? Has a story been assigned? Scheduled? Timing for follow-up calls varies by

type of media. Expect to talk to a lot of voice mail. Don't expect to get calls back. Daily newspapers and broadcast media can be followed up in one to two weeks. National magazines, except for news magazines, work four to six months ahead and have longer decision cycles.

Many writers and editors pile all the incoming mail until they have passed the deadline for the issue they are producing. They want you to go away and stop bothering them; they say they'll call if they're interested. (Maybe, but it helps to have them pull your press kit out of the pile.) Some editors circulate material and have editorial meetings to decide on what they'll use. A decision can easily take a month or two.

7. Make more follow-up calls. You'll need a system for keeping track. I print out a page from the "press" database for each AA and A media, and put them in a ringbinder. With each call, I make notes to track progress. Anticipate making a minimum of five calls. Editors who give you a straight yes or no are great, but sometimes you never get an answer and have to analyze for yourself when you are doing reasonable follow-up and when you have become a pest.

8. Over a period of time your follow-up list will have a bunch of "no thanks," several specific issues for which your story is scheduled, and some "maybe in the future, but not now." You may have a few "this is a really stupid idea" responses, too.

How to Pitch a Story

If you are using press releases already, have you ever tried to "pitch" a story another way? A press release or press kit is not always the answer. It is perfectly fine to send a reporter or editor a story "pitch," which simply alerts them to a situation that may make an interesting story. It should be no longer than one typed page.

A pitch can begin, "In your coverage of small and home-based businesses there may be a story in how we came to start (your business), the state's first and only company providing (your service) to (your clients)." Or, think of an interesting angle about your business. Is it rags to riches? Small company competing against the giants? Solving a unique problem?

Be sure your pitch includes who to contact, phone numbers, possibilities for photos or video (yes, photo ops), and other useful information.

These "media alerts" can sit around in files for months before they surface in a story on your subject. But if you aren't in the file, chances are you'll be left out. It is also a good idea to call the media in advance to find out who is covering your subject area, so you can send the pitch to the right person. That can be the beginning of a relationship. The occasional press release on your business, directed to the same person, will pay off in the long run.

Finally, don't hesitate to use the direct approach. If you get a chance to meet a reporter at a business event, walk up and introduce yourself. The reporter is probably working, so don't bog him or her down, but if you have an idea for a story or are willing to be quoted as an "expert" on a topic or two, volunteer. Get the reporter's card (yes, they have business cards) and follow up with a note. When you do get to work with the press, remember they operate under the tyranny of media deadlines. Understand the time constraints and work within them.

A Good Little Thing to Do

Every day, perfect little pieces of publicity run that pay big dividends for someone. Several years ago I was trying to build a membership base for a non-profit organization. Working with their staff and a freelance artist, we created an excellent booklet of very useful information for people interested in the subject area, and offered the booklet for $1 through a mailing and a press kit. One of the publicity placements was the "What's New" page of a national Sunday supplement—one of those little magazines you get with your Sunday paper. The story was only two paragraphs long, but it had two essential ingredients: a strong proposition (the so what), and the price and address. In the first week, we received more than 4,000 orders. Over time, these inquiries were sent membership information and became members at a higher rate than any other source of prospects.

So, if you can create a useful and attractive piece of information about your line of business and use it as a vehicle to attract prospects, think about it. It should not be a marketing piece, it should be useful and demonstrate you are an expert. It should have high production quality so it appears to have high value. Use some color. It is the beginning of a relationship with your prospects and allows you to make a powerful first impression.

Chapter 5

Clinching the Deal
Proposals and Agreements

*"The snow is gone; trees swell with sap.
In no way can my proposals fail."*
—William Warriner, 101 Corporate Haiku

When I started in business I rarely wrote proposals. Now, almost every project involves developing a proposal of some kind. You may not be writing proposals at all or be in a business that will never require them, but maybe you should look at them as a new "marketing arrow" that can help you grow your business. I started writing proposals when I learned that people who were waffling about going ahead with a project—or using me to do it—would always agree to look at a written proposal. If it was a good proposal, I got the business. Some were simply one page long.

Honing your proposal writing skills can help grow your business in two additional ways:

1. In situations where proposals are required, better proposals win more business. Writing proposals is hard, time-consuming work. Losing is a waste of time. If you do lose, try to get to see your competitors' proposals to find out how they beat you.

2. You can compete for bigger projects, because competitive proposals are usually required for the most lucrative business. Often, this means partnering or work-linking with another small business that allows you to round out or complement your skills.

If you have been writing proposals you may agree that it is a skill much like playing a musical instrument: No matter how good you get, your performance is rarely perfect and there is more to learn through practice and experience.

The Unasked Questions

Whatever the subject area, I begin with the premise that proposals should succinctly answer a client's often unspoken four primary questions:

1. **Do you understand my problem or need?** If you have listened carefully and asked questions during the initial meeting, you will understand. You can prepare an opening paragraph or two of the proposal (called a situation analysis) that describes the current situation.
2. **Can you solve my problem or provide what I need?** This covers two issues: your specific experience in situations similar to the client's (hopefully with a record of success), and your plan for this prospect.
3. **Why should I believe you can do it better than your competitors?** Your client list, letters from satisfied customers, and your biography are all part of the answer to this question. If the project is a big one, you may have to partner with other firms, so you must build their credibility, too.

    You may be at an advantage because your client knows he or she will be dealing with you, an experienced principal of your firm. Some companies have a sales team come in to make the pitch, but ultimately the client deals with other people who are at the periphery during the pitch. The project may actually be turned over to newcomers who are still on their training wheels in the business. Clients suspect this and may be more receptive to your personalized service.

There is also an odd dynamic between clients and suppliers about other clients. They like to know about your successes with past clients, but it is usually a mistake to say too much about your current clients. The client wants to feel secure that your undivided attention will be focused on their situation. If there is someone else in your life, they don't want to know about it.

4. **How much will it cost?** Unless a client asks for a lot of breakdowns, which may be the case in government contracts, the budget is a place to be brief and to the point. One sentence is adequate unless more information is requested. A description of how payment is to be made can be included in that sentence: "The work described in this proposal will cost $30,000, with payments to be made in three equal parts beginning with the signing of the contract."

There is a difference between *having* something and *buying* something. *Having* solves a problem or meets a perceived need. It is the happy part of the deal. *Buying* something is pain because it implies paying for it. It is for good reason that when you are in a jewelry store the diamond is the star, and the price tag is tiny and upside down.

Developing a Price

You will arrive at the price by estimating how long it will take you to perform each component of the job, how much you will spend on travel, and how many expenses you will incur (phone, production of documents, materials, special equipment you must buy, etc.) that are over and above your normal overhead, which is built into your hourly rate. Developing a cost for a large job is like eating an elephant—it must be done one bite at a time.

During this marketing phase of a business relationship you normally spend several hours meeting with clients, writing proposals, and making presentations. These hours should be recorded and built into your proposal to compensate you for your time. Often, development of a proposal involves the most important analysis and strategic thinking of the entire project.

The proposal writing process can be simplified or complicated (depending on your affinity for new computer programs) by "project manager" computer software programs. These allow you to build costs in phases and print them out as multi-colored charts, which look very impressive in a proposal if skillfully done.

Although the proposal should not include all the details of the price, be prepared to back up your price with the specifics of how you calculated it. You can prepare a spread sheet, which will both provide the details and allow you a point of reference to monitor your actual costs and compare them to what you thought they would be when you wrote the proposal. This comparison is valuable for managing the current project and for doing a better job on the next proposal.

The Meeting Trap

It is easy and costly to underestimate the amount of time you will be required to spend in meetings with the client. People (particularly managers) in government and large corporations spend much of their lives going from one meeting to another. Meetings become an end unto themselves. You may be asked to come and present to your prospective client. But someone up the corporate structure may be too busy to attend, and because the function at this stage may be to gather consensus so no one (except you) gets canned if your project goes sour, you will have to come back and do it all over again.

Meetings have no dollar and cents value for people who collect checks every month for mostly just going to meetings, but they certainly have a dollar and cents value to you. It is a tough sell to convince someone that you are going to charge them $100 an hour simply for sitting in on a meeting. But don't be meetinged to death. Be specific. Be clear about how much time you are prepared to spend in meetings, and exactly when you will begin charging for meetings that go beyond the scope of your proposal. And be aware that this will be tough to enforce when you are issued a purchase order for a fixed price based on your proposal.

I have a love/hate relationship with proposals. Most of the time I know the proposal is necessary to demonstrate competence and win the work. But I also know that the most creative strategic thinking will go into developing a solution to a client's problem, and I'm handing it over for nothing as part of the "action plan." No question, clients have tossed our proposals onto some staff person's desk and said, "Here, we can do this ourselves." I only know of one, an attorney, who has done so successfully. To protect yourself, focus on *what* will be accomplished rather than on *how* it will be done.

Sample Proposal Outline

In the four questions discussed above, I have hinted at an outline for a proposal to provide services. Following is a typical outline, which can be altered to reflect your type of business. Shown below are some examples of a hypothetical proposal to conduct research and make recommendations for a national organization that has been experiencing a threatening decline in membership.

I. Situation Analysis, or Overview

This overview consists of one or two paragraphs showing your insight into the problem that is to be solved, the need that is to be met, or the opportunity that will be seized, from the client's point of view.

> The Society of Octogenarian Hang Gliders is facing a decline in membership that has averaged 11 percent annually for the past six years. The resulting decline in dues threatens the financial stability of the Society, and reduced participation has shifted the workload to fewer and fewer members. The Board of Governors has declared that reversing the decline is the organization's top priority, and has embarked on a three-phase program of research, review, and implementation. This proposal describes a research program designed to uncover the causes of the decline and produce concrete recommendations to revitalize the Society.

II. Objectives

This is a crisp, numbered list of what you hope to accomplish for the client during the project.

> To fully understand both the problems and potential for the Society, we recommend a research program that will:
> 1. Identify the market potential for the Society through demographic research into the number of octogenarians involved in hang gliding nationally, whether this market is growing or shrinking, and at what rates.
> 2. Uncover internal policies, procedures, or practices that may be deterrents to growth.
> 3. Evaluate the effectiveness of membership marketing materials and activities.
> 4. Establish the level of satisfaction or dissatisfaction of current members, and identify problem areas.
> 5. Evaluate the perceptions of the Society among individuals who are not members but meet all membership criteria.
> 6. Identify marketing messages that resonate among qualified nonmembers and should be included in marketing materials.
> 7. Develop specific recommendations for action based on our research findings.

III. Approach

This is not included in every proposal, but is used when there is a special situation like a short deadline or where important decisions must be made about setting priorities.

> Recognizing the precipitous decline among existing members, we propose beginning the project by conducting focus groups with current members in four key regions of the country. For reasons of economy, we will concurrently conduct focus groups with nonmembers and then turn our attention to other objectives. Information gleaned in the qualitative research in the focus groups will be used

to structure a telephone survey for the quantitative research phase, which involves calling more than 800 individuals.

IV. Action Plan and Timetable

The action plan is an overview of the major phases and a client's deadlines, which may be connected to the payment schedule. Be sure to include here, or in a separate section, exactly what you must have from the client in order to accomplish the task. This can include access to people and places at specified times, new or existing research, plans or blueprints, specifications, or work that is being done by the client concurrent to your work. This is a good place to mention that work will begin only after you have received a signed letter of agreement, purchase order, or contract. It also should be clear about when the project will be considered finished. The action plan is connected to deliverables, Item V.

Phase 1. Background and Planning

- Meet with the Board and staff at National Headquarters to become familiar with the organization and its operations,
- discuss all concerns and understand Board and staff opinions on causes,
- collect marketing materials and review membership operations, and
- gather information for drafting moderator's guides for the focus groups.

Timetable: The first Board of Governors' meeting after a letter of agreement is signed.

Required from the Society: Membership rosters, past and present, for focus group recruiting. Also needed is
- Tour of National Headquarters,
- Current and past membership marketing materials, and
- Meetings with membership personnel, governors.

And so on.

V. Deliverables

These are the reports, findings, recommendations, designs, illustrations, surveys, studies, or whatever you give to the client. Often deliverables include a preliminary or draft version and a final version, and deadlines for each. In some situations the final deliverable is a presentation to a client group along with supporting printed material.

> April 1: Draft copy of the moderator's guide submitted to the Board and staff for comment and approval. Ten days allowed for review.
> April 15: Final copy of moderator's guide submitted to the Board and staff. Focus groups, April 20 to May 15.
> June 1: Reports on findings from the Focus Groups.
> June 15: Draft of questionnaire for telephone survey for comment and approval. Allow 10 days for review.

And so on through the project.

VI. Budget

Keep it short. Be prepared to defend it. Specify your terms for payment.

VII. Attachments

Attachments often have to do with you and your business and are used to build credibility. They can include your company's qualifications, your biography, a list of past clients, letters of appreciation from past clients, and anything that demonstrates you are uniquely qualified to perform the work in the proposal. Those involved in design or the visual arts can make this their portfolio section.

Once prepared, this kind of material can be stored in your computer and customized and updated as necessary. To customize it, focus on projects that have a bearing on the proposal at hand, and downplay or eliminate items that do not relate. I have five different biographies in the computer, each focused on a different aspect of the business.

A Final Word on Proposals

There are as many ways to write a proposal as there are to bake a cake. If someone you know wins a lot of business through proposals, ask them if you can see one. A friend who is a space planner and designer brings clients "idea books" of materials she sketches and copies from dozens of sources she scours through. By listening carefully, she knows what will excite her clients.

For one presentation, a group I was partnering with wrote and produced a music theme for an advertiser and handed out tapes after playing it. We also had our written proposal, but the music was so memorable that we won the account. A few years later someone else beat us. As part of their pitch they had buttons made up bearing the slogan they were proposing *and* theme music.

Find out what works for you, and constantly try to make it better.

Troubleshooting

You may have already run into some common problems that can be avoided by paying attention to the details of proposals, agreements, and the ultimate working relationship between you and your client when the project is underway. Here are six problem areas I've experienced:

1. Avoid discounting your fees on someone else's terms. If you choose to offer someone a discount because you see an advantage (a huge project that will keep you buzzing all summer when things are normally sleepy) or because you want to give a break to a non-profit organization, that's fine. Beware, however, of the client who asks you to lower your rates because

- their financing hasn't come through just yet, and/or
- there is going to be a lot of work for you in the future if you play ball with them now.

A slight variation on this theme is the claim that someone else offered them a break or a more competitive rate. If you've done your homework on your fees, that should not be an issue. Discounting your rate does two things for you:

1. It sets your rate for all future projects with that client. It is a tough sell to convince your client that you can't continue to do work for the reduced rate, because you have just been doing it. People who promise rewards in the future have short memories. When the time comes to increase your rates, they will probably go to your competitors, claim they weren't satisfied with your work, and try to con them into working at a discount.
2. It lets your client know you are easily conned, a process that will now be part of every discussion. You and your work have been devalued.

As you may have observed, these clients often become clients from hell. They will "lose" your letter of agreement or try to make their deadline problems your deadline problems while they ignore the letter of agreement. Ultimately, they may never pay you.

2. Have you become careless about getting letters of agreement? Even those business relationships that began so amicably can present problems. A common problem is that your original client contact moves on and someone else comes in that knows nothing about the agreement and doesn't honor it. Even people who made the agreement together may see it from different points of view as time goes by. Get it in writing.

3. Do you understand your new client's payment system? In large, restructured organizations, your client may not understand the accounting department's requirements, especially if your client is new to his or her job. Payments can be delayed if someone forgot that a purchase order and accompanying number is required with the billing. Ask your client for the name of someone in the company's purchasing or accounting department, and volunteer to find out what is required to get the ball rolling.

4. Do you tend to get stampeded? In an effort to be flexible and cooperative, it is tempting to begin work on a project before all the paperwork is processed. Someone else's deadline problem becomes your problem, and you may find that the work you have done before the paperwork is signed is ineligible for payment. This is particularly true of government projects. It is another reason to check with the client's purchasing or accounting department and ask specifically about the starting date under company ground rules.

5. Do projects go on forever? Understand when the job is completed. Define what you will deliver, and when, in your letter of agreement.

6. Are you being caught by midstream changes? This is called "contract creep," and it happens all the time, quite innocently (or, sometimes, deliberately).

You've probably run into situations in which the scope of services you are expected to perform expands without considering additional compensation for your efforts. Our business has a couple of these problems going on right now with a year-long project funded, indirectly, by the federal government. Our deadlines are passing, but the contract has to be signed by the governor of a state. His office only reviews these once a month, and the paperwork wasn't before him in time for the previous session. The contract clearly states our company won't be paid for work done in advance of the approval. And while it was being negotiated, we were asked if we would be willing to conduct marketing workshops in conjunction with another part of the project. This is the time to say: "Yes, we can do this, but it is work beyond our original agreement." Write an addendum to the agreement with additional compensation included.

Get It in Writing: Letters of Agreement

Are you currently using a letter of agreement? When you're starting out and doing business with people you know well, projects often are done on a handshake. But as you grow and begin dealing with larger, more distant, and less well-known clients, you'll want a more binding document of understanding.

If you are using a letter of agreement now, it is worth a review from time to time to see if it includes all the provisions necessary to avoid any problems that have popped up as surprises in the past.

If you don't have one, a standard letter of agreement takes about two minutes to prepare and can save hours of anguish and a great deal of money. It pays for you to take the initiative because you get to clearly spell things out on your terms, and clients will usually go along with your terms if they are reasonable.

I have used the letter of agreement in Figure 5.1 for public relations projects for more than a decade.

You can adapt this sample letter of agreement to fit your business, or another option is to go to an attorney and have a "standard" letter prepared for your field of endeavor. Or, write it yourself and have an attorney review your draft. It should cover:

- What you are going to do for your client. If you have written a proposal and it has been accepted, you can refer to it as a basis of understanding.
- How much you will be paid, and on what schedule. Now is the time to cover any special terms like: 2 percent will be added to accounts due past 30 days, or 2 percent discounts can be taken for payment in ten days.
- Expenses you plan to mark up (if any) and how much.
- The method by which you or your client can get out of the deal.
- When the project is to be completed. This could be a fixed period of time, completion of a "deliverable," or some other recognized benchmark.
- What you expect from the client, either in terms of resources, information, or their response to your critical deadlines.

FIGURE 5.1 Sample Letter of Agreement

> This letter, when signed by representatives of MarketReach and *(the client)* will confirm that you have retained us to provide public relations services effective *(date)*. This agreement may be canceled by either party with 30 days written notice.
>
> The specific project covered in this letter is the public relations effort described in my proposal of *(date)*. *(If no proposal exists, specify the work, deadlines, and what you expect from or have been promised by the client.)* For our services on this project the monthly fee is $4,500 plus unusual expenses (other than local travel and telephone costs). Expenses over $100 will be approved by you in advance. Production costs such as printing, graphic design, photography, and video production will be marked up 17.65 percent. The monthly fee will be reviewed in six months to determine if it accurately reflects conditions existing at that time. Accounts will be billed on the first of each month. Two percent is added to accounts due past 30 days.
>
> We will perform these services as directed and approved by you. MarketReach will assume information provided and approved by you for general publication is factual. We assume no liability for errors in those facts, or for claims and promises made.
>
> You have our assurance of our very best efforts on your behalf.
>
> _____   _____
> David Schaefer for   (Date)   For (the client)   (Date)
> MarketReach, Inc.

SUREFIRE TIP

Ask your professional society. The letter above is a based on a sample letter of agreement provided by the Public Relations Society of America. Many professional organizations have such model letters, so if your occupation has a society, see if they'll give you a letter.

- The terms of your "fixed fee" or retainer arrangement: "If efforts on behalf of (the client) exceed xx hours per month, those additional hours will be added to the monthly fee at the hourly rate of $xxx."
- The arrangement for obtaining client approval, if necessary, for commitments of money and for travel. Small clients are leery about how you spend their money and how much traveling you are doing.

Once you are satisfied with your letter of agreement, print two copies on your letterhead. Make sure you have two signature blocks, yours and theirs. Sign both of your blocks and send them off with a note to your client asking that they sign and return one copy. If it is longer than one page, initial the pages without signature blocks and ask the client to do the same.

SUREFIRE TIP

You can find a template for a consultant's contract in the "Business Maven" section of the "Home Office Computing" Web site at: www.smalloffice.com. If you have trouble locating it, go to the "Search" button and type in "consultant's contract." The contract template comes from a detailed book by veteran consultant/writer Herman Holtz, *The Complete Guide to Consulting Contracts*, published by Upstart Publishing Company.

Facing the Monster Contract

Once in awhile your client can be a huge corporation or agency of government with a monster "boilerplate" contract designed to cover every possible contingency and federal bidding requirement. If you have trouble understanding it, get an attorney involved. It may involve insurance coverages, bonding, and hiring requirements (among other things) that you simply cannot promise. Federal government contracts often require a "contribution in kind" of up to 20 percent of the total price—that may mean giving up your profit. If you don't want to spend the money for an attorney, try other sources of information. Legal advice is available on the Internet, in computer software, and in legal books for small business. You also may hire an expert in the field to review it for less than it would cost to hire a lawyer. As a last resort, call the client and try to negotiate a simple letter of agreement. Argue that the small business is the new strength of America and you are being deprived of doing business simply because you are small. If you are shut out, call your Congressperson and tell him or her the same thing. Follow up with a letter to the Congressperson, and copy the corporation or agency.

CHAPTER 6

Tune Up How You Charge, Bill, and Collect

"Money isn't everything as long as you have enough."
—Malcom Forbes

One of the benefits of a growing business is the sense of confidence that comes with it. When your home office factory is full, it is time to subcontract some of your work, raise your rates, or both. Raising your rates is one way to screen out clients who have been, or will be, less profitable. You make more for working fewer hours, and, with some experience under your belt, you can begin to employ flexibility in how you charge. For example, because you now have a good idea of how long similar projects will take, and because your experience has improved your efficiency, you may find a flat rate is both more profitable and easier to sell than an hourly fee. And a flat rate takes you out of charging by the hour and becoming a "commodity."

Unless you recently have examined your rate structure and the underlying principles behind it, your rates and the realities of your business situation may be traveling down different forks in the road. It's probably time for a tune-up and some troubleshooting.

Are Your Rates Realistic?

A good time to think about raising rates is when you are busy. You have a choice about whether you raise your rates for all clients, new clients only, or marginal clients. Usually, it is done in a brief letter to clients. If the thought of actually raising your rates makes you uneasy, here are three questions to ask yourself:

1. Has anyone mentioned that your rates are too high or out of line with your competitors? Do you know what your competitors are charging?
2. Because you now have some experience under your belt, have you evaluated your rates recently to see if they still have (or ever did have) a realistic relationship to the costs of doing business and providing for your future?
3. Are your clients pleased with what you are doing for them?

In my experience, the dollar amount of your rates is less important than how people perceive the value of your work. In short, people are happy to pay high rates for solid results, but they are unhappy to pay low rates for poor results.

A Simple Formula for Establishing Hourly Rates

In my conversations with folks who are self-employed I have come across very few who have actually worked through a formula to test the sanity of their rate structure. More often, rates are set to be competitive with the local market or are a best guess at what the traffic will bear for a specific project. Are you leaving money on the table by not thinking through your rate structure? Here's a formula.

First, establish what you want to make in terms of your annual income. Be realistic and avoid making this a wildly inflated figure. Find out the average annual salaries in your field of work. You should want to do better than that, though, because you are good at what you do, you can operate very efficiently, and you are taking a risk by being out on your own. Salary surveys are conducted by trade organizations and publications. Give them a call, or research it in the library (or online) in publications like the *Occupational Outlook Handbook*. Suppose a typical salary in your line of work for someone with your experience is $50,000.

$50,000 ÷ 50 weeks
(you get a two-week vacation this year) = $1,000 weekly

$1,000 ÷ 5 working days weekly = $200 per day

$200 ÷ 8 working hours per day = $25

So the hourly wage before overhead is $25.

Now, calculate your overhead. If you have been keeping track of your expenses, you should have little trouble in determining your overhead and seeing if your rates are realistic. Don't ignore providing for your retirement. The time to do that is now, not later. Here are some of the major categories to consider:

- A retirement plan, such as a SEP-IRA. If you don't know what this amount should be, here's a quick way to get a ballpark figure. Suppose you need $30,000 a year in retirement income to supplement Social Security and any other income sources you will have. Suppose your retirement investment fund returns 10 percent a year. You'll need to have a nest egg of $300,000. It's fairly easy to count the years between now and your intended retirement date, calculate how much you need to stash away each year, and then translate this into a monthly amount you should be investing in a retirement fund. There's more on this in Chapter 7.
- Medical and dental insurance
- Disability insurance, health insurance, life insurance, business liability insurance
- Letterhead printing, supplies, and equipment replacement
- Telephone service
- Your office space, plus heat and light. There's more on this in Chapter 7.
- Self-employment tax, for the privilege of taking all the risk
- Auto and travel expenses
- Memberships in business and professional organizations
- Professional fees for attorneys and accountants
- Advertising
- Entertaining clients

6 / Tune Up How You Charge, Bill, and Collect

- Specialized equipment like pagers, video cameras, or other items necessary for accomplishing your work
- Online services, Internet service provider
- Contract labor, like a bookkeeper

You may have other overhead costs not listed here, so add them up and come up with a monthly total for your overhead. Remember, your overhead is not the same as money you must spend to accomplish a project for a client. Those are direct costs, and they are billed back to the client. The normal direct costs are things like postage and delivery services, travel, printing, and so on. Marketing firms normally mark up production costs like printing by 17.65 percent or more. You should mark up fees for production and services when you must pay for them before you bill them, and are acting in the role of a "bank" for your client. Small direct costs have a way of getting lost and never billed back to the client. I keep notes in my Day Runner, right along with hours, on all out-of-pocket expenses on behalf of clients. The postage meter has a log sheet next to it. They add up. I don't bill every postage stamp or telephone call, but when a client is very active these can add up fast, especially when you start sending things by overnight courier or making international calls.

Next, break down the monthly overhead figure into an hourly figure. Suppose it turns out to be $30. Is your hourly rate to produce an income of $50,000 now the $25 plus the $30 for overhead, or $55? Not quite. By now you know that you will not be billing eight hours a day for five working days every single week. You will be marketing, writing proposals, doing administrative chores, and talking on the telephone—things for which you can't bill. If you're going to build your business, you'll be spending two hours a day marketing. Now that you have some experience, you can go back and check your monthly billings and come up with a reasonable monthly average of the hours you actually bill. This exercise can be very revealing.

Suppose you actually bill only about half your time, 80 hours a month, or four hours a day. It is not unusual to bill only half or three quarters of your time when you analyze it over the long term, one year, for example. If that ratio holds true, you have to double your rates to $110 an hour to make the target income. How does that measure up with your current picture? If you market effectively and increase the number of hours you bill, you can offer lower rates. That's one option if your new rates are way out of line with what everyone else in your area is charging. If business is good, you can increase your rates and make more by working less. There is also a middle ground: Raise your rates in increments and increase your hourly billing to reach the target.

Other Ways to Bill

With a year or more of experience under your belt, you may want to reconsider how you bill. You have many choices and can use a variety of them to suit individual situations.

Hourly rate. This is the most common way to bill, and probably the method you are using now. Some consultants argue you should never bill by the hour; hourly billing turns you into a commodity. Instead, you should structure a project price based on the value of your work to the client's organization. That is good advice for certain situations, but many requests for proposals (RFPs) require you to not only identify your actual hourly rate, but also to report a ratio of hourly rate to overhead. The federal government, for example, requires this kind of breakdown. In large organizations, overhead may be three to five times the hourly rate shown for the individuals assigned to the task.

This sounds confusing, but it's consistent with the formula for establishing rates. If and when you worked in a service company, your salary was probably one-third or less of what your company billed you out for. And you darned well better be billing out at least seven hours a day to *someone*. The "creativity" of the billing process in some organizations is legendary. Here's an anecdotal example:

> An advertising industry billing joke: The creative director of an advertising agency dies and arrives at the pearly gates, where he is met by an angel with a clipboard. "Name?" the angel asks. "John Smith," he replies. "Oh, yes, here's your record," says the angel, flipping through the clipboard. "Let's see, your age is . . . ." "I'm 73," says Smith. "Oh, that can't be," the angel replies. "I have your hourly billing records here—you'd have to be at least 106."

6 / Tune Up How You Charge, Bill, and Collect 81

Over time, it's tempting to get casual about keeping track of those small direct costs you incur on behalf of your client, things like mileage, postage, copying, small purchases, and courier services. If these expenses are slipping away, for each client write the client's name and month on a No. 10 envelope and keep the envelopes on your desk or, while traveling, in a briefcase or over the visor of the car. Having all the receipts and notes on mileage in one place makes all the difference in keeping track of small expenses. Some judgment is required at where you draw the line. Billing a client for 12 cents for copying looks like you are nickel and diming, and you would be. But a consolidated item for copying, postage, courier services, and long-distance phone charges can be justified.

Billing your time for travel on a client's behalf ultimately comes down to a judgment call. If you travel 15 minutes each way to attend a meeting with a client, do you charge for that time? If you travel an hour each way to attend that meeting, do you charge for it? When you worked for a company, did it dock your pay for days spent traveling on the company's behalf because you weren't actually grunting over your desk producing something? If you don't charge, it is lost time because you can't be doing something else—another one of the factors that reduce billable time. Many companies bill travel time at half the normal hourly rate, plus expenses. My own practice is to forget about short trips and marketing-related trips, but bill half time, and in some cases full time, when travel is required to perform the work. For example, recently I completed a project that required driving all over the state on ice-slick roads to conduct one-on-one interviews with legislators and journalists. Schedules switched during the day and I had to check in hourly by cell phone with the person scheduling the interviews. The total interview time was four hours, but I charged full rate for the full day I spent running around. In a variation on this theme, if you have to travel plus pack and unpack a lot of equipment to do an hour's work, it's time to think about a fixed price or billing in half days.

When you buy goods or services on a client's behalf it is common practice to mark them up, so if you haven't been doing this you are leaving money on the table. The percentage varies by profession or occupation or industry. The local carpenter may charge you an hourly fee and add 10 percent or more to the cost of the

FIGURE 6.1 Sample Invoice

Invoice

Public Relations Services for March, (year)

Hourly fees @ $95 per hour:
3/4 Develop custom press list of software magazines	6.0	
3/5 Draft #1, Basic release and fact sheet	5.0	
3/6 Review meeting with marketing staff	3.0	
Total	14.0	$1,330.00

Expenses
3/6 Mileage, 42 @ .31	13.02
3/12 Printing, 200 presentation folders	222.67
Copying, postage, courier, long distance	27.00
Total	**$1,592.69**

lumber he purchases for your project. If you've ever been in a hospital and been billed for each aspirin, you know the cost there has nothing to do with the cost at the local drug store. I mark up production costs, like printing, photography, and graphic design, and in the advertising industry the accepted rate is 17.65 percent.

In video production, the production houses give me a producer's discount—a rate not available to the client—so I charge for my hours but do not add another markup to their retail price schedule. If you are uncertain, you can simply mark up those items that you must pay for even if your client never pays you. You are "the bank" in that case, and are taking a certain risk.

Whatever you plan to mark up, make sure you have specified it in your letter of agreement so there are no misunderstandings down the road.

Common computer programs, even word processing programs, offer templates for billing. I simply record hours and expenses in my totally interactive (paper and pencil, always with me, no batteries required) pocket organizer, and provide my clients with a thorough itemization after the first of each month. I have never had a bill challenged. A typical but fictitious bill looks like the one in Figure 6.1.

Reviewing How You Bill

Whatever method you currently use for billing, it is worth critiquing it from time to time to see if you've outgrown it or need more flexibility. One reason for a review is profitability: now that you have experience, you may come upon a formula that makes better financial sense. A second reason is the marketing aspect. An alternative method of charging may help build the business. The auto industry is an interesting example. Not long ago, almost all individuals bought and owned a car. Now, leasing is an attractive option. Would one of these alternative billing techniques make sense for you?

Hourly, not to exceed a given amount for an entire project. This means you bill your hourly rate at what you think it will take to complete the entire job. Be clear about whether or not expenses are included in this negotiation. If you miss the estimate badly, you eat the hours and costs. Be careful and draw on your experience. On the brighter side, it could be the kind of arrangement that gets you started with a new client who has a fixed budget. Be sure to keep track of time and expenses on such projects, which are rare, so you can learn from the experience and adjust future quotes accordingly. Normally, the client has gotten a deal, but these can be profitable if you can draw on resources you may have created for others in the past, like background facts, press lists, computer modeling, and so on.

Hourly, in phases. Phase one may be a fact-finding or research phase. Phase two could be implementation of a program on a limited basis. Phase three may be a full program. This allows clients to control expenditures and make decisions based on experience. Your job is to upsell to each new phase, and more, bigger and better phases. Obviously, it is better to get the whole project in one shot, and that is how you should propose it. Phases can be a way to break the ice and get the project moving, so keep them in mind for negotiating.

Half days and full days. Businesses such as video production companies charge in half and full days because they really can't afford to pack the gear, travel, shoot, and unpack for just a few hours on location. If your work for a client involves a lot of travel between short bursts of work, consider billing by half days and full days.

By the project. This is similar to billing by the hour with a "not-to-exceed" price. Sometimes the budget is set by the client, and you are tempted by it because it is summer, things are slow, and you are hungry. The more experience you have, the better prepared you are to do project work profitably. You can run into problems if there is more to the project than meets the eye. Sound familiar? Once the price is fixed, clients like to slip in additional work for the same budget. Speak up, and help stamp out contract creep. If you are adept and work quickly, pricing by the project can be very profitable.

Flat rate. If you sell the same kind of service over and over again, you know how much time and materials it will take. Preparing a will, producing a small ad, writing a press release, clipping a pooch, even researching and scripting an eight-minute video can be done on a flat rate. Services that can be provided in a predictable single visit or two are possibilities for flat rates.

Fixed fees, or retainers. A fixed monthly fee makes sense for advertising agencies and other service businesses who perform best when they are intimately familiar with all of a client's needs, problems, and opportunities. It is also a good way to have a client dump you if you haven't been doing much. ("What are we getting for all this money, anyway?" someone will eventually ask.) Usually, however, there is a continuing level of activity on the client's behalf that justifies such an arrangement. For example, if you and the client agree that you need to spend x number of days per week or month working on their behalf, that time will become the basis for setting the fee. One of the selling points to use with clients is the predictability of the budget.

Discounts for large projects and non-profit organizations. Everybody loves to get a bargain, and you always have the option to offer a discount—say 15 percent—for jobs that will keep your plate full for a long time (particularly if just hourly fees are involved). You also can provide a discount for non-profit organizations, if you wish.

Piece rate. A flat rate applies to services, and a piece rate is used for charging for tangible items such as illustrations, word processed letters, banners, and so on.

Deferred, contingency, speculative. Some work is done speculatively in hope of a reward later, often a greater reward for taking the risk of not getting paid at all. Obvious examples are writers who write a book or magazine article on speculation and hope to sell it. Attorneys have the option of taking a case on "contingency" instead of charging hourly rates, hoping they will share in a large court award or settlement. I have helped people write business plans with a written agreement that I will have some equity in a new venture and capture all of its public relations business. I usually regret these decisions, which are always made during slow periods.

Except for the piece rate, I have used every one of these methods at one time or another to meet the needs of the project type or the client.

Billing Cycles

Have you ever been caught in a cash flow crunch while you wait for your monthly bills to work their way through a new client's payables machinery? A simple cure for that problem is to negotiate different arrangements with a client. This should be done up front in the initial negotiation. Some examples include:

- One-third/one-third/one-third. You can negotiate to collect one-third up front, another third at a significant benchmark at the midpoint, and the final third on completion.
- Half up front, balance on completion
- Barter or trade out your services for goods or services of equal value

Collecting from Clients from Hell

It would be unusual if you have been in business for awhile without having to deal with a "slow pay," and from time to time with a "no pay." Your three alternatives for action can actually be handled as three consecutive steps that turn up the heat by degrees:

1. Appeal to the client's sense of decency and fair play. It actually works sometimes.
2. Become a determined telephone nag.
3. Turn it over to a lawyer or collection agency.

Two issues that usually cloud these situations are:

1. Whether or not you will continue to do business when the client gets back on track.
2. The amount of money involved. The few times I have been stiffed, it has been for amounts in the $1,200 to $1,700 range—and most of it has been for hourly fees. A lawyer can chew through that amount in fees in no time, but the small claims courts in your area might offer an alternative.

"I say, old chap, I'm not a bank, you know." Although a few people really do operate on other people's money and seem to thrive on it, most businesses get behind because they are waiting for someone to pay them, or they are going through a slow period. You know how that can be. But sometimes checks actually vanish into thin air. If clients who are usually prompt suddenly become very slow, call sooner rather than later. I have had clients find my checks under their postage meters, and I got one envelope months late, all chewed up and black, looking like it had been caught under a conveyor belt in the post office. Today, for instance, I have been on the phone with someone in a federal agency who swears a check was mailed from 100 miles away two weeks ago. For some reason, only checks vanish; bills never get lost in the mail. In this case, I asked that they issue a stop payment on the old check and issue a new one. Don't be shy about asking people to send late checks by overnight courier. In most large organizations, you'll find the accounting people helpful and accommodating.

Often, though, the problem with small clients is a cash flow crunch. While you may be sympathetic with that problem, you can't afford to work for clients who don't pay, so take action. First of all, it is likely that a lot of people are lining up to be paid, and you should not be silent if your bills are going well beyond the time allotted in your letter of agreement. Now is when you will begin to be glad that you have a letter of agreement. Second, your client would like to be treated just as you would like to be treated under the same circumstances. Before the telephoning for payment begins, try writing a letter to your primary contact (not accounting) that appeals to his or her sense of fairness. Here's a letter that has worked for me on more than one occasion:

Dear John,

We've really enjoyed working with you over the past few months, and I believe we've made substantial progress toward our objectives. I've noticed, however, that we've badly slipped behind in the payment schedule outlined in our letter of agreement and I thought I'd better call it to your attention now rather than later.

We certainly understand cash flow issues and hope you're just having a temporary setback. As the smallest of small businesses, we are severely impacted when clients get behind in their payments. Unlike large corporations, we are paid personally only when our clients pay us in a timely manner. We can't afford to be placed in the role of a "bank" for a company many times our size. I hope our relationship can continue, so I'll call you a week from today to discuss our options.

Sincerely,

A letter like this can at least get your invoice moved toward the top of the payables pile, if your contact has the desire and power to set such a priority. A week is enough time to have a check drawn, and it is certainly enough time for you to get a call back with an explanation or plan. Those of us who provide business services normally have much more personal relationships with our clients than other suppliers, and this fact alone can often break the logjam.

"When can we expect a check . . . ?" One of the unfortunate parts of working alone is that it is hard to play good cop/bad cop. In a regular office you, the noble employee, could leave the nasty chore of calling the client's bookkeeping department to a secretary or someone in accounting. But as a home-based business proprietor, the dirty work is up to you.

Here are a few tips for turning up the heat:

- Call at random times, and ask when you can expect a check. Some states have ruled that calling every day constitutes harassment, which is prohibited under fair debt collection laws. Every state has a consumer protection agency that can furnish you with your state's collection laws.
- Make notes about the time, date, and outcome of your call, and about any promises made about payment. Suggest paying off in installments.
- If a check does not come, call more often. Be polite and profoundly disappointed that the promised check hasn't arrived, and suggest that you will take action through legal channels.
- If a check is promised, and the client is local, tell them you'll pick it up in person, and you are on your way over.

One day I sat with a long-time business associate, waiting for a television crew to show up because he had filed for Chapter 11 bankruptcy at his prominent business. "It isn't fair," he said, "but the bums who nag you all the time are the ones who get paid. They simply wear you down."

Getting Outside Help

As the situation progresses, investigate your options. You can try the consumer protection agency, but it doesn't occur to most folks to turn to them in a bad debt situation. Consumer protection offices usually work out of the governor's office or the state attorney general's office. In large population areas the agency may work on a county basis. They will be able to provide information on:

- Small claims court. These are courts for individuals, designed to help people recover small amounts of money due them without having to hire a lawyer. There is a ceiling to the amount involved ($3,500, for example, but it varies by state) and a schedule of modest fees for processing. Small claims court is one reason to keep records and notes of your efforts to collect, and now you will be very happy you have a signed letter of agreement or contract with your client. You file a complaint, the defendant is notified, and the process begins. A hearing will take place if no negotiated settlement is reached.
- Fair Debt Collection laws in your state. These vary, but the basic federal laws apply only to people collecting for others, like attorneys or collection agencies. States have adopted their own versions that also may apply to you when you are collecting for yourself. For example, you may be restricted from calling people at home instead of the office. Do not threaten clients. It's worthwhile to actually speak to an attorney about a situation before telling a client you plan to take legal action. If you go too far, you may be breaking the law.

The consumer protection agency also can tell you whether or not there are other complaints about your client. Simply ask if they have any. The agency maintains a record of complaints against specific businesses for a variety of consumer-related problems. In our state, car dealerships and home repair problems top the list of complaints, and you can find out which dealerships and repair firms have logged the most complaints.

If all else fails, you must decide how much you are willing to spend to collect the amount involved by going on to civil court or retaining a collection agency. Pull all your invoices, correspondence, and telephone notes together and go to your attorney. He or she may fire a warning shot across your client's bow by writing a letter on the firm's letterhead informing the client a law firm is now on the case.

Collection agencies will take a percentage of what they collect, ranging from 25 to 50 percent. They might charge an hourly fee or an up-front fee. Check the yellow pages under Collection Agencies, and ask other business people for any suggestions or recommendations. Collection agencies begin by trying to determine if there is something to go after, something to attach. They begin by doing their research.

And therein lies the moral of the collection saga. If you are unsure about your potential client, you can save all this trouble by doing some advance research through the consumer protection agency or asking around the business community. The credit bureau only provides information to its members.

SUREFIRE TIP

Visit the morgue. If they are open to the public in your community, and many are, the files of your local newspaper, called the "morgue," are a great source of information. Individuals and businesses have files of clippings that trace most of their public history. This is how reporters get background on today's news events, and it often can give you a clue about who you are dealing with. More and more of this information is available on line. Check with the libraries in your area. You can do a lot of research by checking news clippings from your computer, or looking through online business information services.

Chapter 7

Make the Most of What You Earn

*"Anybody can make a fortune.
It takes a genius to hold on to one."*
—Jay Gould

*A*re you surprised at where your money goes now that the initial start-up costs are behind you? Insurances, telephone bills, and, of course, taxes are unrelenting drains. It pays to revisit them from time to time to see if you can do better. Credit card interest rates are another area worth a review.

Insurance: How Much Risk Can You Tolerate?

Insurance looms as one of the most expensive categories on the business horizon, but it's a topic that makes most people's eyes glaze over, until something goes wrong and raises the haunting fear that whatever went wrong is the one thing excluded by the policy. And many self-employed simply take a risk; surveys show 14 percent don't carry health insurance.

Because there is so much to do when you work alone, one common and potentially costly situation is failing to review your insurance to see if it matches your current needs. Are you paying auto or health insurance premiums for teenagers who are now off on their own? Are you adequately covered as a home business?

Because individual situations vary so widely, I will simply provide a few "heads up" items to stimulate thinking about various insurances.

1. Did you know that your business activities and equipment at home probably aren't adequately covered by your homeowners insurance policy? Are you aware that your computer, the furniture, and other equipment you're taking as business deductions may not qualify as personal property covered by your residential insurance? A client visiting your home on business might trip over the dog, break a leg, and look for their right to be made whole again. You may not be covered. Business insurance is relatively inexpensive, but the cost of replacing everything uninsured and lost to a flood or fire or theft may put you under.

Check with your insurance carrier to see what is covered. Usually you can get a rider on your homeowners policy that will cover your business needs for $100 a year or less. Some policies will cover lost income caused by a home office disaster, but they will cost more. If your business relies heavily on intellectual property stored on computer disks, inquire about coverage. At the very least, back up your data frequently and keep a backup copy of the most important information in a safe deposit box or some other location away from your home office.

If you are a road warrior and carry cameras, a laptop, or other expensive electronics, be sure they are covered and do the obvious thing: permanently identify them with an engraver or permanent marker.

Business insurance policies are like menus. You can order extra provisions to meet your specific needs, so think through how you work and what you will need to recover from a mishap.

2. Are you getting the best deal on health insurance? The health care industry is in turmoil, but one thing is clear: It pays to shop around. If you took the COBRA option and continued the coverage you had under a former employer, you probably can do better by shopping around. Get several quotes. In Appendix B, you'll find a list of home-based business organizations that offer insurance. Find out which state agency is responsible for regulating health insurance in your state, and ask them what kind of information is available to help you make a decision. You can learn a lot about Health Maintenance Organizations by asking the consumer protection agency in your area about complaints they are receiving. Other sources of information are the attorney general's office or consumer divisions of your state's health insurance regulators.

3. Do you have, or need, disability insurance? This is the kind of insurance that provides income if you are injured or sick and unable to work. In the past decade, disability insurance has become a tough proposition. Many highly paid professionals (doctors, for example) have filed for disability for big dollars. Several insurance companies have gotten out of the disability insurance business. A few have taken it on and taken it over. Prices have soared to the extent that some professionals would rather take the risk of being uninsured than pay the premiums.

People who work at home are at a disadvantage because it is difficult for an insurer to march into your home workplace and establish whether or not you are really out of commission or just dogging it. Insurers also are skeptical about small new businesses with no financial track records. Again, get quotes from business, professional, or other organizations that will put you into a "pool." A critical question to establish in your discussions with potential insurance carriers is: How disabled is "disabled"? Does it mean you can't do the work you are doing now, or does it mean you can't do any work? Ask how likely are you to be able to collect under the various scenarios you can imagine. As an invisible economy, the home business owner is very vulnerable on this issue. If you are laid off from a larger company, you show up in unemployment statistics and can collect unemployment. But if you starve to death while self-employed, you never show up on anyone's radar. You qualify for nothing: no unemployment, no worker's compensation if you get hurt—nothing.

SUREFIRE TIP

Get into a group. The individual is at a disadvantage when shopping for insurance. Your local chamber of commerce or a business or professional society may offer insurance at better rates. Contact an independent insurance agent who can shop around for you. Compare those rates with those offered by the home-based business organizations.

Cut Costs

Long-Distance Rates

Long-distance rates a mystery? If your long-distance bill is more than $50 a month, you may want to check out *http://www.telegroup.com*. This site compares the price of a call from and to locations you determine, for a length of time you determine. It compares AT&T, Sprint, MCI, and Telegroup, which sells long-distance services and sponsors the site. These deals change all the time, and it is important to find out how long the special rates will be in effect. Cases are being reported of telephone rates doubling, unannounced, a few months after signing up for a "deal."

Cut Credit Card Costs

Given the high interest rates, this is the first kind of debt to eliminate. Paying the full balances every month is one solution, but if the balances do creep up at least try to carry a card that has low or no annual fees and low interest rates. To compare the offers of low-rate credit cards, go to the Ram Research Web site at *http://www.ramresearch.com* and click on CardWeb. You can apply for a low-rate card online, or simply read the CardTrak section on all the new things you can do with credit cards. You also can find the current prime rate, which is used as the base for credit card interest rate offers. Comparative credit card information is also available by sending $4 to Bankcard Holders of America, 524 Branch Drive, Salem, VA 24153.

Avoid Scams and Scoundrels

The consumer protection agency in your area is worth another mention. Every state has one, and some have local or regional offices. They can tell you about complaints they have received from consumers about all kinds of businesses, from car dealerships to home repair scams. Our state was one of 19 that went after one of the largest and most aggressive long-distance companies for switching customers to a more expensive calling plan without individual permission. Based on consumer complaints, the attorney general's office threatened to forbid them from operating in the state unless the long-distance company cleaned up its act. If you're offered one of those "too good to be true" deals, check with consumer protection. If you have a complaint, they'll ask you to document it with a brief letter.

Are You Getting All Your Tax Deductions?

There are three major areas to consider:

1. The home office deduction
2. Deductions and benefits that apply to everyone who is self-employed, whether they work at home or not
3. Reducing your taxable income by investing in a retirement plan

The Home Office Deduction

In 1993, the U.S. Supreme Court threw a curve ball at home office workers. The National Association for the Self-Employed estimates that up to 1.6 million entrepreneurs have been affected by a ruling against a self-employed anesthesiologist named Nader Soliman. Dr. Soliman deducted home office expenses for a spare

> **SUREFIRE TIP**
>
> Disqualify the office the year before you plan to sell, because the capital gains requirement only applies to active home offices. This means taking it totally out of office use, not just moving the exercise bike or television back into the room. In fact, while having the bike or television may disqualify your office for a deduction in the first place, simply putting them back in won't disqualify it when you want to change its status before selling the house.

Obviously, home office deductions are tricky, and perhaps even more subject to IRS interpretation than the regulations governing large corporations. The language states the deduction has to be based on "all the facts and circumstances," and that leaves a lot of room for interpretation.

Don't take the deduction if you have any questions at all about meeting the criteria. There is a lot of speculation that the home office deduction is one of the "red flags" that triggers an IRS audit. Sometimes the deduction doesn't warrant the audit risk.

So, if you haven't already, spend some time with an accountant familiar with home and small business issues and you can avoid problems down the line.

Simplify Recordkeeping

Although tax laws change from year to year, one way to make sure you are getting all your legitimate deductions is to set up your recordkeeping program in categories that will be easy to use when tax time rolls around. Setting up these categories in one of the available "checkbook" computer programs will make tax time much easier, because these programs sort all the categories, do the arithmetic, and organize the information so you can export it into a tax preparation program. The software also allows you to write and print checks from your computer, capturing the necessary tax information in one step. In addition to the home office expenses, here's a refresher checklist of nine items you can deduct if they are for business purposes only (if they are mixed with personal use, you can deduct only the business portion):

Business Deductions

1. *Telephone.* You can't deduct the first and only phone line into the house—only the business portions like long distance, call waiting, distinctive ring, etc. Keep good records. Better still, get a business line.
2. *Automobile.* Keep track of the business use of your personal car at 31 cents a mile plus parking and tolls. It will come in handy at tax time to make a note of the mileage on January 1 of each year.
3. *Computers & other equipment.* For business use only, you can expense or deduct up to $18,500 in business equipment (without depreciating it over several years). But you can't expense more than your taxable business income. This amount will increase gradually to $25,000 by 2003.
4. *Meals and entertainment.* Only 50 percent of these costs are deductible. Keep records of who you entertained, the business purpose, and topics discussed.
5. *Travel and vacations.* Business travel is deductible. If you mix business with a vacation trip, travel costs aren't deductible unless the trip's primary purpose was business. You can deduct a pro rata portion of your hotel bill and meals, and any direct business expenses.
6. *Medical expenses.* Talk to your accountant about the possibility of hiring your spouse and setting up a medical plan for employees and their families (you). You can't cover yourself directly. If you hire family members for any reason, their work must be legitimate and documented. You have to prepare all the forms, such as W-4 for tax withholding, W-2 for annual tax purposes, and quarterly 941s for wages paid.
7. *Retirement plans.* These are the best kinds of deductions because they take place "above the line." That is, they are deducted before your adjusted gross income is deter-

mined. Individual retirement account (IRA) and Keogh plan contributions are these kinds of deductions. (Discussed in greater detail later in the chapter.)

8. *Business expenses.* In your computerized recordkeeping system, categorize the major items. These records help you understand what it is really costing to operate your business.

    In addition to those listed on the left, typical categories are:
    - Advertising
    - Outside services (accountant, attorney, consultants, bookkeeper, etc.)
    - Dues & Subscriptions
    - Supplies
    - Printing/Production
    - Taxes—Business, Federal, Local, State, Property, Payroll
    - Education
    - Wages
    - Rental equipment
    - Repairs (equipment)
    - Postage

9. *Health insurance premiums.* You can deduct 35 percent of your health insurance premiums, beginning in 1997. The rate increases by 5 percent per year to 80 percent by the year 2006. Since 1996, under COBRA, you can permanently take your health insurance coverage with you when you leave an employer. (The limit used to be 18 months.) But shop around, you may be able to get similar coverage for a reduced cost.

Don't Overpay Estimated Income Taxes

It is nice to get a big income tax refund in the spring, but, of course, if you have been overpaying during the year, your money is essentially a no-interest loan to the government. You could have been putting it in a SEP-IRA, which allows you to defer your taxes on it.

How do you know how much to pay? The government has a simple formula for calculating estimated taxes and will assess a penalty if you fail to do so. If you made less than $150,000, your estimated tax payments should be 100 percent of the tax shown on the preceding year's tax return, payable in four quarterly installments. Or, you can pay 90 percent of your total taxes for the current year in the four installments. If you earned over $150,000, you have to pay 110 percent of the past year's tax, or the 90 percent of the current year's tax.

SUREFIRE TIP

You may find your federal income tax chores are easier as a result of changes to the tax law. More self-employed people can now use simple Schedule C-EZ to report profits, because the ceiling on gross receipts in now unlimited (it had been $25,000). The amount of business expenses that can be claimed on the form has increased from $2,000 to $2,500.

Planning for the Future

Defer Paying Taxes Until Your Retirement

Funding a retirement plan is not only a good idea for tax reasons. Because of longer life expectancies, you run a real risk of outliving your retirement resources, so it's wise to keep building those resources.

How much do you expect to get every month from Social Security once you have retired? You can find out, and it is a good place to begin when estimating what you have to do to provide for your future. If you're like most people, your income will drop after retirement and you'll pay less in taxes, so the more you can put away for retirement the more taxes you defer until then. If you have been making contributions to Social Security for several years, you can get an estimate of how much you can expect to receive based on your past and current earning patterns. It's called "Your Personal Earnings and Benefit Estimate Statement" and it is available by calling the Social Security Administration at 800-537-7005. It will give you an estimate of what you will receive if you retire at age 62, age 65, or age 70.

A review of your Social Security retirement benefits can be a wake-up call to start thinking seriously about how you will provide for retirement. Talk to your financial planner, banker, or broker about setting up a SEP-IRA or Keogh plan. How much will you need to have invested to make up for a shortfall? A quick look: If you will need $30,000 a year over and above what you get from Social Security and other retirement plans—and investments can be assumed to produce a 10 percent yield—you will need $300,000 in investments.

Beginning in 1997, the Savings Incentive Match Plan for Employees (SIMPLE) provides a new set of options for employers, employees, and the self-employed. Designed for businesses with fewer than 100 employees, a lot of the literature talks about SIMPLE plans from a small business perspective. But it also works for the solo self-employed, and allows you to make contributions of up to $6,000 of your net earned income (income minus deductions) a year. This ceiling will be adjusted annually for inflation. These contributions become deferred income, reducing your taxable income each year. You pay income tax when you begin to withdraw the funds. The SIMPLE plan replaces the Salary Reduction SEP (SAR-SEP). Existing SAR-SEPs will continue, but no new ones can be started.

Normal IRAs have been improved—in families with just one working spouse—to allow both spouses to deduct $2,000 (a total of $4,000) for IRA contributions instead of just a $2,250 total for single-income families.

With conventional IRAs there is a 10 percent penalty for withdrawing funds before you reach age 59½, but with the SIMPLE plan that penalty increases to 25 percent during the first two years of your participation. These plans do not reduce Social Security benefits.

In Chapter 10, you'll find a suggestion on funding a plan with part of the "rainy day" fund.

CHAPTER 8

Financing Your Growth and Avoiding Problems

"I've been rich and I've been poor, and believe me rich is better."

—Joe E. Lewis

*B*orrowing money is a necessary evil in business. If your home business plan is working, you will need some cash to launch your newsletter, organize and promote your seminar, self-publish your book, improve or replace your computer equipment or other tools of your trade, or fund out-of-the-ordinary expenses. Craftspeople, for example, often borrow money for raw materials so they will have plenty of inventory available for a major craft show.

If you are well established and can secure a loan with the equity in your house or other tangible assets, you probably can go to your bank or credit union and get a personal loan to cover your business expenses. But if you are not in that enviable position, financing your growth presents a challenge.

"Banks only want to lend you the money if you really don't need it," is a common complaint, and for good reason. For years there has been a void in available financing for truly small or "micro" business ventures. Business loans for under $10,000 and up to $20,000 have been especially hard to get, partially because banks are among the most regulated of the lending institutions and partially because very small business loans are not profitable for banks. Yet almost a third of all businesses are launched with less than $10,000, and almost 90 percent start with less than $100,000.

Finding Money for Growing a Business

But things are changing in the financing picture, and a bank is not always the best place to turn to. When you start your search, don't inquire about "small business" financing. Ask whether there are financing programs available for "micro business." You'll find this kind of financing is accessible in places you would never have suspected, like your city hall and city, county, or regional economic development authority. You may have to make a few phone calls to find the right group, but nearly every community in the country has some kind of economic development group at work, and they are not just there to help build factories for big companies. Growing small, existing businesses is part of their mission. In fact, these micro loan programs are specifically for very small businesses and, because they are the least regulated of the lending programs, they can make loans other institutions can't touch. Some even provide loans for working capital, the money you need to keep going until the new venture produces a profit.

One organization to seek out is the Small Business Development Center (SBDC) in your area. This is a national program partially funded by the Small Business Administration (SBA). Again, these groups are affiliated with regional industrial development organizations and with state colleges and universities. Although an SBDC may not actually administer the loan, the staff members are familiar with the many kinds of alternative financing that exist, including special programs for female- and minority-owned businesses. SBDCs can provide or direct you to many small business services, one of which can even help you develop a business plan. For SBDC information, check your local telephone book or call 800-827-5722.

Money for micro business financing is often from "revolving loan funds," capitalized with federal seed money and income from the repayment of the loans made. These types of loans are administered by the non-profit development groups through a loan committee, and, unlike commercial lenders, they spend little or no money on advertising, so unless you attend small business conferences where they have information booths or are speakers, you may never hear of them. To find one of these organizations in your area, key in on the words "community development" or "economic development." Once you visit their offices, you'll get a full picture of all the services available in your area, because there are usually several different programs offered through various organizations and they all know about each other.

Here is the profile of an actual revolving "micro business" loan fund operated by a municipal economic development group. To get this loan, you need to go to city hall, not a bank:

- Amount of loan: $500 and up, with no cap. For home-based businesses, the loans are typically between $5,000 and $10,000 and are used to buy computer equipment and set up the office.
- Interest rate: 8 percent.
- Repayment schedule: Up to five years, but prefer payment within one year.
- Restrictions of use: Fixed asset financing, inventory financing, and working capital. (These loans are not intended to help you pay off debt.)
- Equity and collateral requirements: Loan applicants must show they are investing their own time and money into their business. Loans are secured by all business and personal assets.
- Application process: Fairly simple for loans up to $1,500, but increasingly more complex as the amount tops $5,000. Loan application fees range from $20 for amounts up to $1,500, to $300 for loans over $20,000.

Your credit will then be checked out, and you will have to provide cash flow and financial statements on a regular basis, normally every six months.

Business Plans

The application process for even small loans, under $1,500 for example, will require you to fill out a Business Activity Worksheet. For larger loans, you probably will be asked to prepare a "micro" business plan. Business plans have two main sections: a narrative section that describes the nature of the business, your experience, and your marketing plan, and a financial section that projects your income and expenses. The lending office will provide you with an outline of what is required and a few forms. Typically, you'll be asked to provide:

- An executive summary. This is one page that describes the business structure (sole proprietorship for most lone operators), names the principals and location of the business, provides a brief business history if there is one, and explains why you are writing the plan (to obtain a loan for . . .).
- A business description. This describes in more detail who you are, what you do, what geographic markets you serve, the current status of the business, and why you think the business will succeed.
- Marketing research. If you completed the marketing evaluation earlier, much of this section is already done.
- A competitive analysis. You name your direct competitors, and your business position in the face of that competition. Again, much of this is in your marketing evaluation.
- Promotion and advertising strategy.
- A plan of operation. Describe the day-to-day operations, how you will perform the work, and list professional services you are using, (e.g., accountant, attorney, consultant, insurance agent).
- A capital equipment list. A list of equipment your business has and needs.
- An income statement. The same as a profit and loss statement, this is a detailed monthly picture of income and expenses that spans a fixed time, usually a year. Forms are often provided.
- Balance sheets. A snapshot of your financial picture today, and a similar one showing how you expect it to look in a year.

8 / Financing Your Growth and Avoiding Problems

- A breakeven analysis. A calculation of how much work you need to perform, or services or products you must sell, to make money. If you've gone through the work on tuning up your fees, this is already close to done.
- A personal resume.
- Tax returns. Copies of your personal federal, state, and local tax returns, probably for three years.
- A personal monthly budget. A summary of where your household income comes from and goes to.
- A personal net worth statement. An itemization of what you own and what debts you have.
- Other relevant documents. For example, if you are expanding to meet business commitments or contracts you already have in hand, that's important. Letters of reference, leases, and legal documents also can be important.

Rounding up this information looks like a daunting task, and it does take some time. However, if you don't already use one of the computerized money management software programs, this is a perfect time to start. Programs like Quicken, Mind Your Own Business, and others have fill-in-the-blank templates for most of the things you'll need for this type of loan application. Once done, they are always on file and much easier to update for the next expansion and your own financial planning.

The SBA is developing a pilot program for micro business loans called the 7(M) MicroLoan Program. It is available at a limited number of locations, usually in areas that are struggling economically. People at your state's SBA office or the SBDC will know if and where it is available. It is administered by non-profit community development organizations or private contractors involved in community development. Here's a profile of how it works:

- Loan amounts: $100 to $25,000, with the average being $10,000.
- Interest rates and repayment: Rates are pegged at no more than 4 percent over the prime rate, with up to six years to repay.
- Restricted uses: Machinery, equipment, fixtures, leasehold improvements, and possibly receivables, and for working capital.

- Collateral: Requirements will vary because the non-profit lending organization has some latitude, but it will include any assets purchased as well as the personal guaranty of the business owner.

Would you really be able to get a loan for installing computer equipment in your home business or for a venture like launching a newsletter or publishing your own book? Hard assets such as computer equipment are fairly easy to finance. A loan for publishing your book would be possible, but a little more difficult and you would have to show a detailed marketing plan and cash flow projections. Another area that is becoming more difficult to finance is working capital for software development businesses. Because software is primarily intellectual property and not a hard asset, there is little to secure these loans. Their default history has been shaky.

If you are a "big" small business and going for small business financing through a bank, the business planning requirements will be substantially more detailed and complex, but the basic outline would be the same. Small Business Administration loans are not actually "made" by the SBA. They are guaranteed by the SBA to the commercial lending institutions. With the downsizing of the federal government, the trend is to provide more decision-making power to the local bank or regional development organization by training small business loan officers.

When the time comes to develop a full-fledged business plan, pick up one of the software programs designed specifically for writing business plans. These programs guide you through all the steps, and often begin the sentences you must complete. You may have to modify a few things to meet the specific requirements of the lender, so ask your contact if they can recommend a software package that meets all their requirements.

Other Sources of Money

One advantage of using the kind of micro loans described above is the forced discipline of a payment schedule connected to your business venture. But home-based businesses frequently finance their activities in other ways. Some of these include:

- *Home equity loans.* This is one of the most frequently used methods of finding capital. Working with your home mortgage holder, you can borrow against the value you have built up in your home. Home equity loans make sense if you can pay them off in a few years and you do not stretch them out over the life of your home loan. For tax purposes, you can deduct interest on up to $100,000 of debt on home equity loans. If you fail to meet the payments, however, your home can be foreclosed.
- *Insurance policies.* If you don't need a lot of money, look into borrowing against the equity you have in your life insurance policy.
- *Lines of credit.* Small businesses frequently rely on a bank line of credit to pay for services or materials they purchase in advance to accomplish work for a client. Your line of credit from a bank can be relatively easy to get if it is in the $3,000 range. It may simply be a special credit card with a low limit. You pay it back when your client pays you. This is the kind of thing you mark up. American Express and larger banks are offering corporate credit cards with lines of credit that range up to $35,000, but you will be paying premium interest rates and must examine your own ability to deal with credit.
- *Your own investments or savings.* Many brokerage accounts offer loans at slightly above prime rates, secured by your investments. This is an easy way to take advantage of a nest egg without actually tapping into it. The disadvantage is the need to establish the discipline to pay it back on a regular basis.

You always can use your credit cards, of course, but I will leave you with one anecdote passed along to me by the local SBDC manager. While working through some loan paperwork with an applicant, they came up with the fact that the individual had 15 credit cards and $60,000 in credit card debt. "When we put it down on paper, I could see a look in his eyes—he just realized for the first time where he stood. I think he'd have shot himself on the spot if he'd had a gun."

When You Grow and It Shows

Working alone and quietly from your home office, you don't attract much attention. But when you grow, it often shows up in the form of remodeling projects or more people coming and going. When you begin to grow and attract attention you can run into some surprises, especially if you have been operating a home business in an area where zoning prohibits business operations.

Here are some red flag areas:

- Generating a business income at home
- Engaging others for services; being engaged for services
- Public access to the building
- Improving land for business
- Beginning nonresidential use of property

Red Flag #1: Generating a Business Income at Home

Zoning is one of the problem areas most common to home businesses. Do you know if you are currently in violation? Zoning ordinances, which are usually accompanied by a map that shows what is permitted in what areas, are available from city, village, or town clerks, or from your municipal planning commission. In an effort to protect legitimate concerns about maintaining the residential nature of a neighborhood, zoning often goes farther than it needs to.

Zoning is not consistent from community to community, and it seldom makes provision for the number of jobs that are now based on managing information. However, old zoning often protects those who worked at home when it was passed—farmers.

Condominium associations also may have specific restrictions against home businesses, as does the one in which I live and work. However, because I'm around most the of the time to deal with tradesmen and other association issues, I was elected president.

Take a close look at the zoning ordinances that control what you can and cannot do in your home. Here's a model "safe harbor" zoning section for home businesses that was developed by the state of Vermont to recognize the interests of home businesses:

Protection for Home Businesses: No regulation may unreasonably infringe upon the right of any resident to use their dwelling for a business, that business being secondary to the principal or residential use of the premises. Regulations may address: a threat to health or safety, the nonresidential appearance of property, significant increases in traffic, or the creation of noises, smells, or lighting that is unusual to a residential area. Regulations shall not:
   A. Restrict the portion of a dwelling to be used for home business.
   B. Restrict the use of existing outbuildings.

It is important not to be arbitrary in home business zoning, but at the same time it is important to protect the health, safety, and welfare of residents and avoid creating a nuisance. Perhaps by suggesting an ordinance like the one above, you can help your community resolve zoning issues to everyone's satisfaction.

Red Flag #2: Engaging Others for Services; Providing Services for Others

The question of who qualifies as an "employee" and who does not can cut both ways. It comes up when you hire services, and when you perform services for others. Is the person who comes in once a week to do your books and pay the bills an employee? What if the business grows and he or she spends three days a week working for you? Is it now an employer/employee relationship? This can be important because it determines whether or not you will pay workers' compensation and it has jurisdiction over whether or not you must comply with the federal Occupational Safety and Health Act.

Now put the shoe on the other foot. If you are providing long-term consulting or other services to a client, and you're around so much they provide an office, are you an employee? This raises a host of issues, from your home office tax deduction to your retirement planning.

Not surprisingly, this question is of great concern to people in the contract or temporary employment field as well.

States usually defer to the U.S. Department of Labor, which has primary jurisdiction over defining employer/employee relationships. Creating a clear definition of what constitutes a temporary or contract employee is one of the items that came up at the White House Conference on Small Business in 1995, but it still has not been adequately resolved to everyone's satisfaction.

A commonly used test, although it may or may not be supported in specific wording in state legislation, is called the "ABC" test:

> "Worker" and "employee" mean a person who has entered into the employment of an employer, where the employer is unable to show that:
> A. the individual has been and will continue to be free from control or direction over the performance of such services, both under his or her contract or service and in fact;
> B. the service is either outside the usual course of business for which such service is performed, or outside of all the places or business of the enterprise for which such service is performed; and
> C. the individual is customarily engaged in an independently established trade, occupation, profession, or business.

The test may not give you a perfectly clear answer about your bookkeeper without knowing more about the rest of his or her business, but it will help you ask the right questions. Even drafting a consultant's contract that claims you are *not* an employee carries no weight if you fail the ABC test.

Remember to file a Form 1099-Misc. each year for all unincorporated independent contractors who you have paid more than $600 during the year. Many of us who work at home—writers, designers, photographers, consultants—are not incorporated. Consistent payment of 1099s helps to define your relationship with your independent contractors.

Red Flag #3: Public Access to the Building

Many additional rules, regulations, and costs can land on the doorstep of the home business which conducts an activity that causes it to be designated a public building. These rules and regulations range from meeting more stringent safety criteria to providing special access facilities for the disabled. Environmental regulations may be triggered when a household jumps to public building status.

The law varies widely from state to state, but some of the red flag activities are buildings in which people are employed or entertained, offices in which two or more people are employed, and day-care operations. There are varying definitions of what portion of a building must be open to the public before it becomes a "public building." You may have noticed that, on one hand, you are encouraged to have clients visit your home office to qualify for the home office tax deduction, but overdoing it may cause you to become a "public building." Your city or town clerk can help you locate the laws that apply in your community. Often they reside in the Zoning Board or Planning Commission.

Red Flags #4 and #5: Improving Land for Business and Beginning Nonresidential Use of Property

These are potentially triggers for setting off the regulations mentioned above. For example, by trying to stick to the letter of the home office tax deduction, and creating a separate entrance for the few clients or customers who may visit, your building permit could trigger a nonconforming zoning use. Hanging out a business sign or storing equipment in a residential neighborhood invites a reaction from the neighbors. And while the home business tax law would encourage you to meet with clients or customers at your home, increased traffic may make neighbors wonder if whatever you are doing is in conformance with the zoning.

There is one other area that doesn't normally apply to service businesses, but it is worth mentioning in case you are involved in some kind of processing (in Vermont, home-based specialty foods like relishes are a big business) or an activity such as restoring antique cars or building custom furniture. When the production of waste water or solid wastes exceed what is "normal" for a household, or when your business causes the release of vapors, you may be crossing a line into a wide range of state and federal environmental regulations that require expensive upgrades.

Some states have developed exemptions for small-quantity generators of solid waste, but if your business produces wastes, releases fumes or materials into the air, or stores hazardous wastes (the cleaners under your sink might qualify), get the facts ahead of time.

And Now for the Good News—Government Wants to Help

The real growth in American jobs since 1989 has been in businesses with 0–4 employees, which means many of these new jobs are solo work-at-homes. This phenomenon is hard to ignore, given the level of publicity and the boom in advertising to the home worker.

As these red flag issues surface across the country, legislatures and communities are dealing with them. Government bodies want to know more about the depth of the work-at-home movement and its impact. In rural states with an attractive quality of life, home-based businesses can be a major source of growth, and many regional development groups and chambers of commerce have special programs and information packages designed to attract work-at-homes. The micro loans are just one example.

CHAPTER 9

Get Organized

"But how can this be?
My Teacher commands me: Press ENTER to exit."
—William Warriner, 101 Corporate Haiku

In every survey I've read about work-at-homes, the items at the top of the wish list are always growing the business, adding some electronic or telecommunications tools, and getting organized. This makes me feel better, because I was worried that I was an underachiever in the world of organization.

But in many years of working in home offices—some of them dingy places right out of Edgar Allen Poe's stories—I've concluded that one simple troubleshooting step can go a long way toward solving your home office organization and layout problems: Get the storage and production areas out of your primary work space!

Most home offices, because they usually evolve rather than result from planning, confuse the working space with storage and production space. For example, copying and collating, stuffing envelopes, storing supplies, affixing postage, printing computer output, and sending and receiving faxes are all production tasks that relate to each other. You print the letter, make a copy for the file, put it in an envelope, affix postage, and put it into the mail basket. Multiply this by 50 or 100, and you need flat work space for collating and stacking. These production functions should be far enough away from the business functions—phoning, meeting, working at the computer—not to interfere.

Zone Your Office for Efficiency

In laying out a home office, you can take a lesson from how good gardeners landscape their property for efficiency. They have zones. The herb garden is just outside the kitchen door, because fresh herbs are used in cooking just about every day. In winter, you'll find them on a sunny kitchen window sill. The flower gardens are within sight of the living quarters, and convenient to cut for a bouquet for the table. A small salad garden may be right behind the herb garden, ready to furnish lettuce, tomatoes, and cucumbers for each day's salad. Farther away, the vegetable garden. And at the back of the property, the fruit trees and berry bushes, which come into season just once a year and don't call for daily visits.

In the home office, the zoning also depends on frequency of use. Try to imagine your work space set up in zones of concentric circles, like a bullseye target. Starting at the center, you can arrange five zones:

1. A work zone of constantly used tools
2. A production/communication zone
3. A materials zone for frequently used references and files
4. A production zone for handling mailings and storing supplies and dead files
5. Possibly a "get out of the office" zone

Kate Keough is an interior designer and space planner who has worked on projects that range from designing the interiors of Saudi palaces to making the most of existing space for businesses and municipalities. Figures 9.1 and 9.2 are a bird's-eye view and a floor plan of her office, which is only eight feet wide.

The storage units are six feet high to make maximum use of floor space. Some are wall units divided into cubes. Wicker baskets and boxes fit into the cubes to collect clutter. The work

FIGURE 9.1 Bird's-Eye View of a Home Office

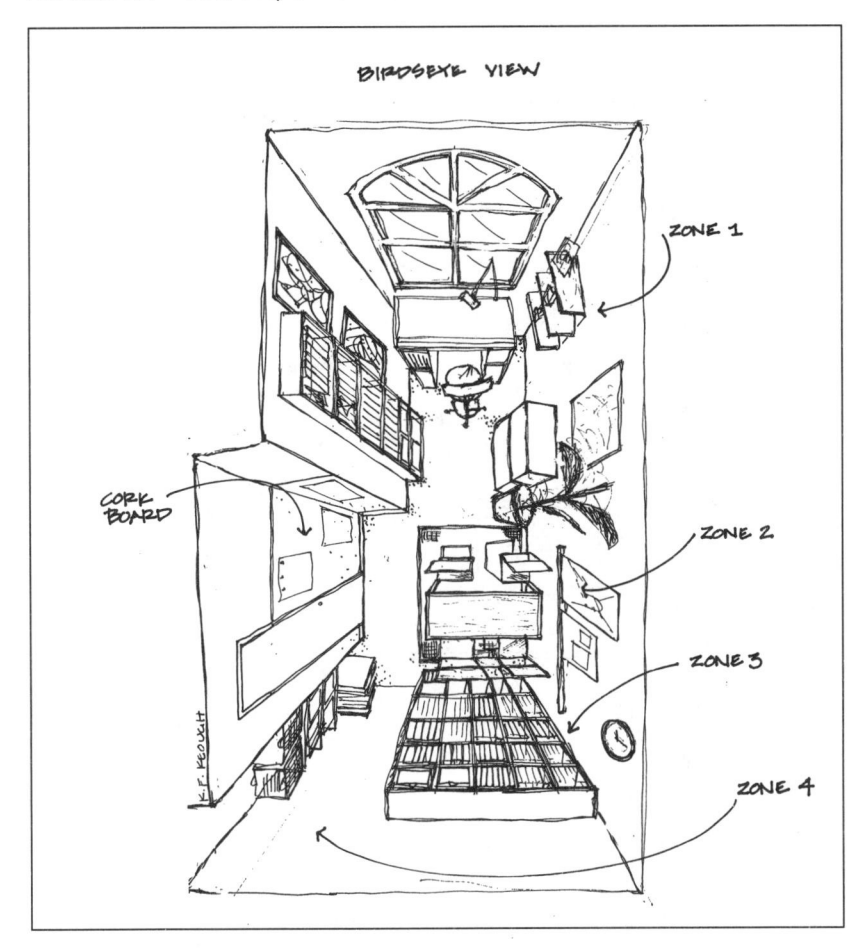

spaces have task lighting and everything is portable. The most expensive item of furniture is the ergonomic chair. The table for meetings and production work came from a used furniture store. Let's further examine the five zones:

1. **Zone One,** for an information worker, is the basic work station. This zone will include the telephone (probably a portable, so the phone is handy wherever your roam), the computer (but not necessarily the printer), pencils and small desk tools, and a place for working files (stored in vertical holders, not in piles). You may want to try a "sus-

FIGURE 9.2 Home Office Floor Plan

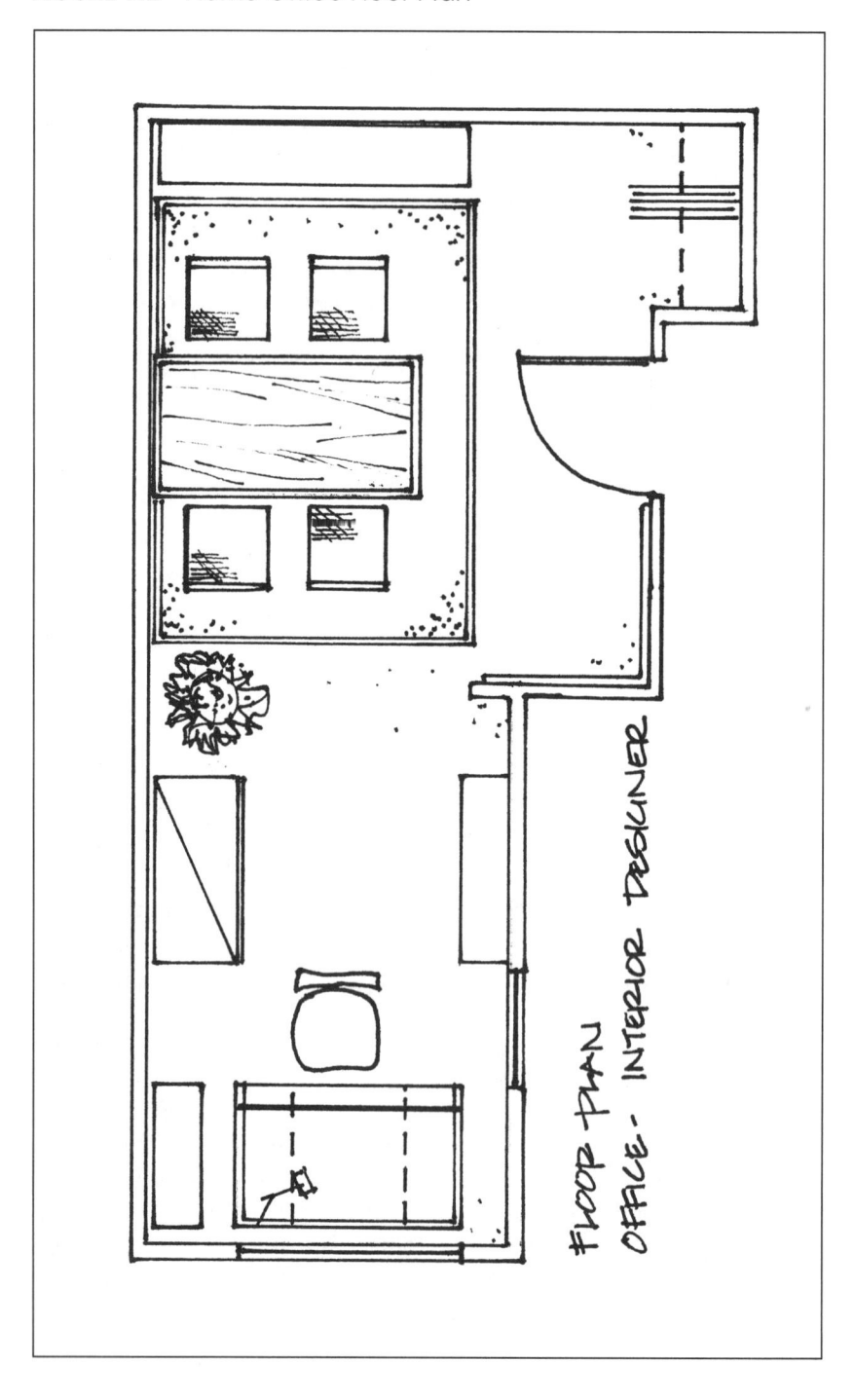

pense file" in the form of an accordion-style book called an "Every Day File and Fast Sorter." It contains papers, files, and notes sorted by day of the month, such as copies of marketing letters that need follow-up.

Zone one should have two kinds of lighting (plus natural light). Kate uses a light with a halogen bulb directed at the work surface. Designers call this "task" lighting. The room itself also should be lit with "ambient" lighting, such as track lighting. The task lighting should be about three times brighter than the ambient. Studies show using task lighting alone can make you feel isolated and depressed.

2. **Zone Two** is a production/communication area. It can include the fax machine, computer printer and shelves for printer paper, letterhead, and supplies. Fax and printing operations tend to be noisy and messy and require a lot of supplies. A nearby closet can be turned into a fine little production center, keeping adequate supplies at hand. The door also can be closed on the mess.

3. **Zone Three** is for materials used less frequently—computer manuals and reference books, more files, and so on. It can be a place for rolling file carts that are pulled up to Zone One when in use.

4. **Zone Four** doesn't exist in every situation, but will be found where the business involves producing bulky proposals, assembling press kits or mailings, and similar work. It is a production/storage center, with a flat work surface, and other facilities such as binding equipment for proposals, old files, and bulk supplies. It's best if this is a separate space, not part of the working office at all. The kitchen table is often a substitute for this zone.

5. **Zone Five** only can be called the "I'm sick of the office" zone. This is one of those small luxuries associated with working from home. You can pack up and move out to the deck or patio for tasks such as reading reports. With a cellular phone and a notebook computer, this zone can be anywhere. When planning your office, follow the rule of "less is more." The less you have in Zone One, where the real work is done, the more you are likely to accomplish. If you haven't used something in a week, it doesn't belong

in Zone One. If you haven't used something in a year, think about throwing it away. Client files and financial records are exceptions to the "one year and toss" rule. Former clients have a way of coming back just when you think they are gone forever. And if you should have the misfortune of a tax audit, you'll wish you had seven years of financial records on hand.

SUREFIRE TIP

Color-coding files. There are many techniques for color-coding filing systems, but I always forget what color represents what concept, with one exception. With the start of every year I change the color of the little tabs that stick onto manila file folders. It's a quick way to sort active from inactive files and to categorize what work was done when for those clients who have projects only every few years.

The same is true of storage. You do not need to have the files or supplies you use infrequently taking up valuable work space in your primary or secondary work zones.

SUREFIRE TIP

Best thing for under $1. I keep a stenographer's pad near the phone for taking notes and recording voice mail messages instead of taking phone messages on random slips of paper. Date each day. With these notes and phone numbers you can reconstruct when conversations took place and easily retrieve phone numbers you never thought you'd need again, but suddenly can't live without.

Finding More Space

Kate Keough also offers some tips gained from her own experience on finding additional storage or work space.

- *Behind a door.* If a door is located near the middle of the wall, the space that allows the door to swing fully open, plus a few extra feet, may be the perfect spot to create storage space. Build a wall as shown in Figure 9.3 and buy or build work and storage areas to fit behind it. The secret is to design it to use every available inch of vertical space for files and storage. If you don't like open storage, hide it with a folding screen, one of those self-standing hinged affairs you can find at import stores. If you are handy, you may build one that has a cork board for messages, or storage on the back. If not, use the back of the door itself, as shown in Figure 9.4. Catalogs like "Hold Everything" have behind-the-door hanging file storage units.
- *In a closet.* Cleaning out a closet could provide a storeroom or office that can be closed off and out of sight when not in use. Closet organizing systems can be used to provide space for office materials and files.
- *Create a space with vertical storage units.* When space is scarce, go vertical with storage units or wall-hung storage. You can create a room within a room with tall bookshelves, but be sure to anchor them to a wall with an L-bracket so they don't tip onto someone. Open storage tends to be a mess, but it can be organized with interesting wicker or paper-covered storage boxes. High-quality wall units are available from stores like Ikea or Techline and the Container Store (see below). The mail order places listed below specialize in solving home office equipment and storage problems.

The Trunk Trick

You can hide a drawer full of hanging files (as well as the kind of flat artwork you have for brochures) in an old trunk that will fit into your living space. I modified an old trunk I bought at an

FIGURE 9.3 Build a Wall to Create Storage Space

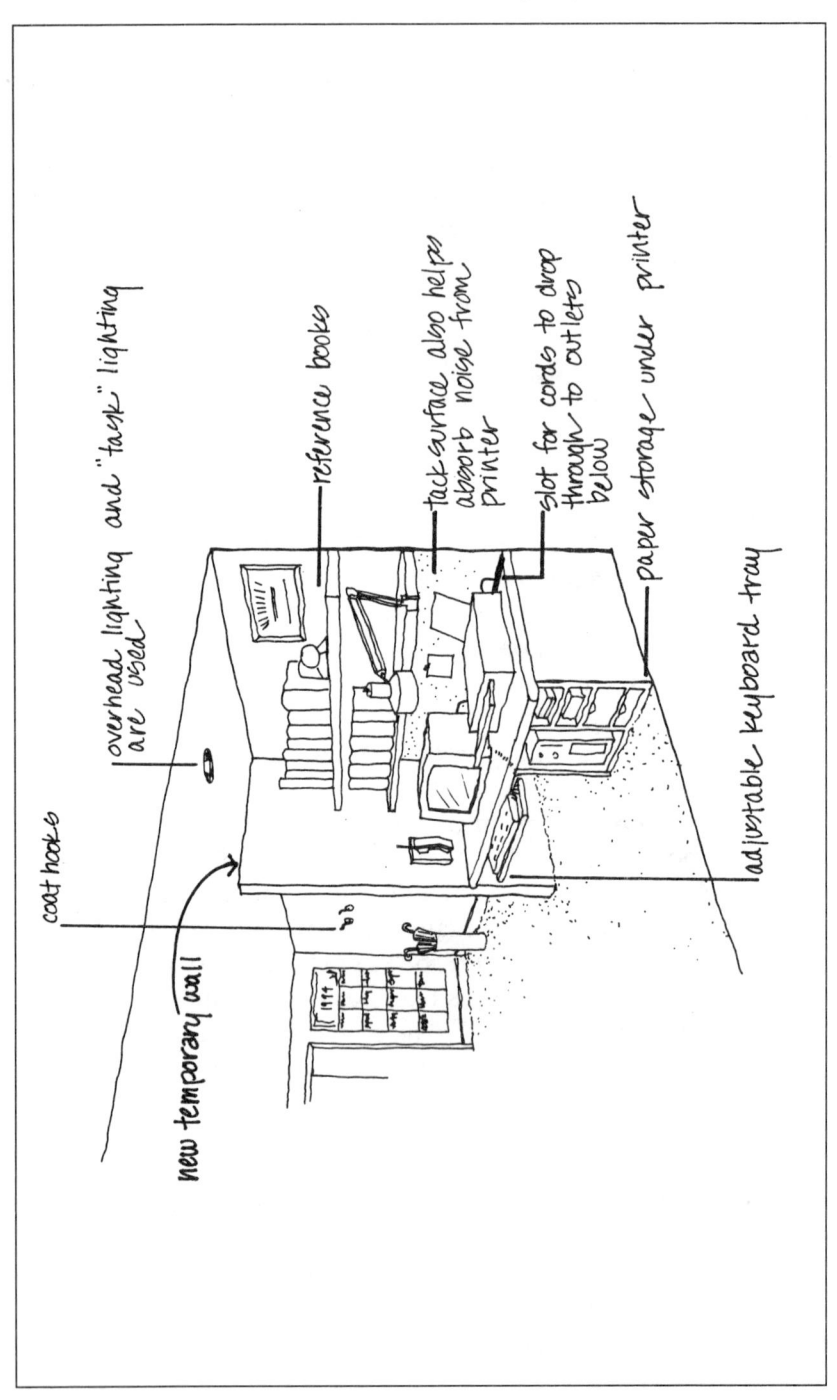

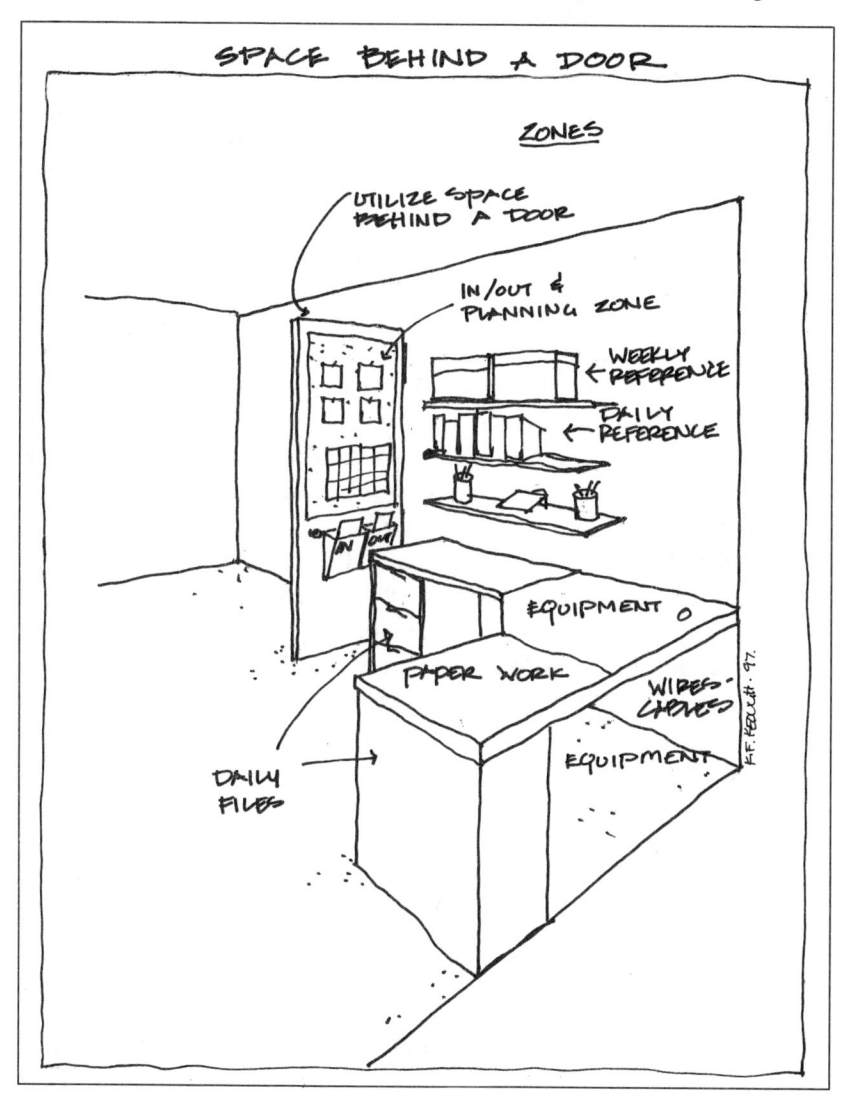

FIGURE 9.4 Utilizing Back of Door for Messages and Storage

auction for a few dollars by attaching wooden cleats to each end and installing L-shaped aluminum tracks at the proper distance apart to support hanging Pendaflex files. (See Figure 9.5.) Some old trunks already have wooden cleats where a shallow tray fit on top of the bulky storage below.

Sources of Interesting Ideas, Equipment, and Solutions for the Home Office

- **Hold Everything.** For a catalog, call 800-421-2264. Organizers and storage for the home office, home, and travel. Nice little boxes for hiding clutter are available here.
- **The Container Store.** For a catalog, call 800-733-3532. Although focused on organizing closets, their storage systems by Elfa also are shown in home office applications. The Elfa system uses coated wire baskets of varying depths that slide into rack systems, which may be a good solution for people like designers who work with bulky projects rather than just sheets of paper.
- **Reliable Home Office.** For a catalog, call 800-869-6000. Furniture, equipment, and storage solutions for the home office.
- **Techline.** For a catalog, call 800-356-8400. This line of high-quality, melamine-laminated furniture was spun out of an architectural firm in Madison, Wisconsin. Wall systems, storage units, and work surfaces of all shapes and sizes can be combined to create an entire room. Very contemporary modular systems. One of their markets is medical cabinetry, but they also focus on the home office (and this furniture doesn't make you feel like you should bend over and drop your shorts).
- **Herman Miller.** For information, call 800-646-4400. Herman Miller is a top-quality furniture design/manufacturing firm that has done extensive research into the home office by "intervening" in the homes of 40 telecommuters. The company provided three different groups with regular office furniture, off-the-shelf stuff sold as "home office" furniture, and the designs the company was testing. This evolved into two lines of home office furniture named with the initials of the designers (the contemporary JB Collection and the natural cherry wood TD Collection). Its Relay furniture line features a rolling storage unit called the Puppy.

  Herman Miller focuses on marketing to large companies for telecommuting solutions, but can ship to individuals through a distribution relationship with Sears. The

FIGURE 9.5 Turning Old Trunk into File Storage

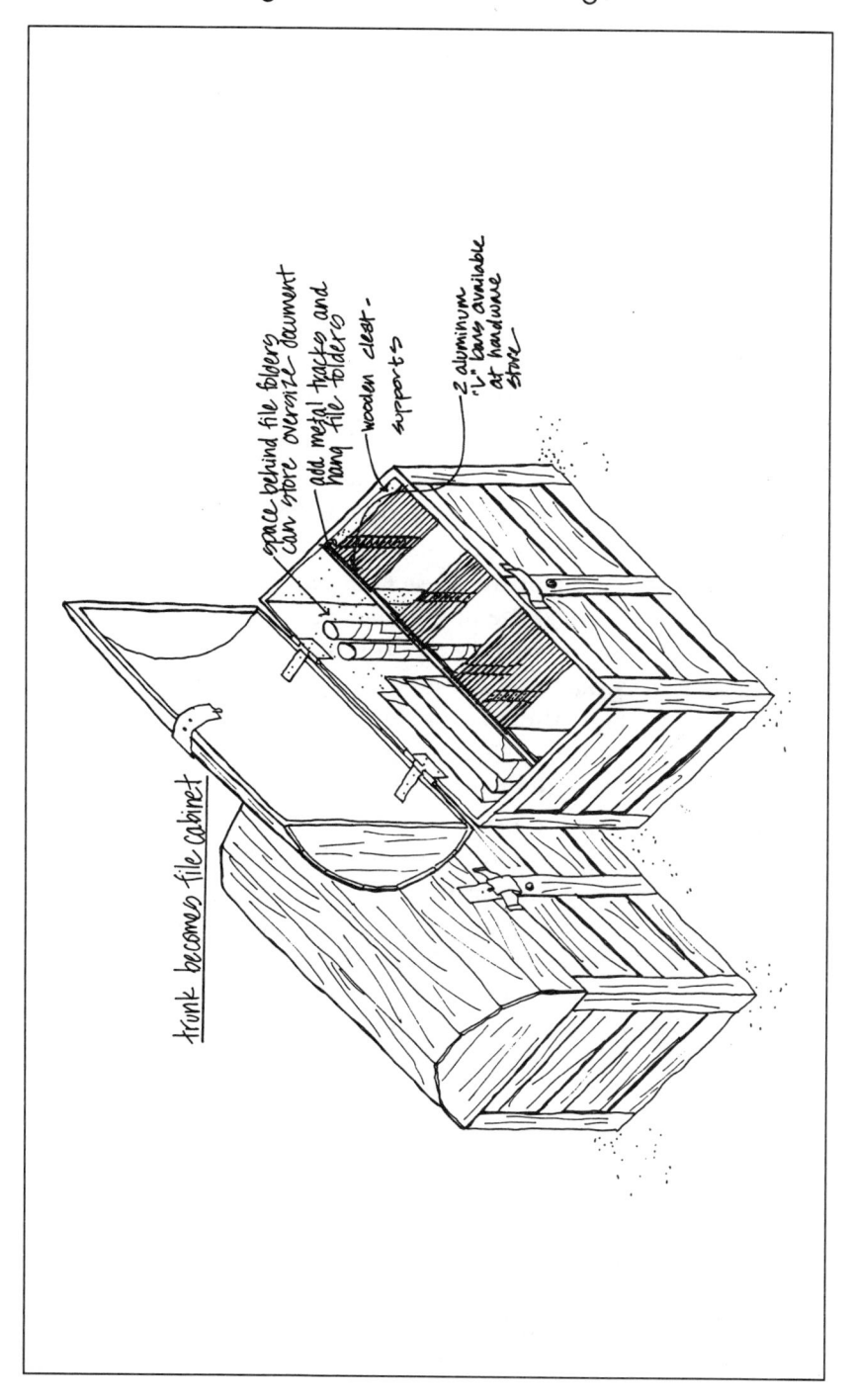

Liaison Cabinet System features storage units that are finished both front and back, so they can be used to carve space out of an existing room. These folks are really good.
- **Steelcase.** For information, call 800-333-9939, or go online at *http://www.steelcase.com*. You actually talk to a real person when you call this number. As a leading manufacturer of office furniture for industry, they have many, many options in their catalogs, including a line for home offices.
- **Knoll.** For information, call 800-445-5045.

Organize Your Telecommunications

Of all the places not to skimp, telephones are the first one. After the initial office setup, your phone system is normally the first place you have to invest in business growth. Of the three marketing goals for a home business—accessibility, visibility, and credibility—telephones are at the heart of accessibility and credibility.

Telephones used to be so easy. You had your choice of colors (as long as it was black) and your choice of features—the rotary dial. In the old days, the rule of thumb was: one line for every three or four employees. Now, with the world online, it is more likely you'll need two lines just to handle simultaneous demands for phoning, faxing, and using your computer's modem.

Don't hesitate to contact your provider of basic phone services to see what they have available for small or home-based businesses. Special customer service centers and newsletters for home-based businesses are available in some areas, along with a Market Extension Line, which combines features of both a business and residential line by providing yellow page listing at lower-than-business rates.

The Dreaded Business Line

Sooner or later you will not be able to get by using a single line because it is tied up all the time with phoning, faxing, and online services or the Internet. Do you need a separate business line?

Your local telephone company no longer acts like the "telephone police," trying to ferret out people who are using residential lines to run a home business. You simply cannot be listed in the yellow pages unless you have a business line, and now even the white pages are being segregated into residential and business listings. So you can be listed as a residence or a business, but not both under the same number in both sections.

Here are some advantages of a business line:

- You can leave a businesslike message on your voice mail or answering machine. No one else has to answer it.
- You are listed in the business white pages and, if you wish, in the yellow pages.
- You don't have to listen to messages left for your teenagers while you are standing at a pay phone or paying top rates from your cellular phone.
- You can add an in-bound toll-free number.
- You can deduct it from your taxes if it is used only for business calling.

SUREFIRE TIP

Make your residential line do double duty. With a telephone company product that provides a distinctive ring, you can have two or three different numbers on one line. My residential line has my home number and my fax number, which makes it look like a dedicated fax line. This line also is used for the modem. The setup leaves the business line free for voice calls. The distinctive ring service requires a special box, available for about $80, and it is often marketed as a way of identifying teenager calls as opposed to grownup calls. The distinctive ring service, called Ringmate in the East, is available almost everywhere.

The disadvantages? If you have never paid for a business line before (one of the benefits of working for a company), be prepared for a shock. It will probably cost you about twice as much in monthly fees and (in some service areas) minute-by-minute charges as an identical residential phone sitting next to it. Services like voice mail and Ringmate also cost substantially more on business lines. Finally, when you add a new business line you'll be faced with reprinting business cards, letterhead, brochures, and so on to bring people up to date.

SUREFIRE TIP

Special telecommunications gear. Want to turn on your PC or jacuzzi by phone? Need one of those little lights to alert you when you have a message on voice mail? Need specialty phones, or a phone/computer system? Want a black box that will route your calls anywhere in the United States? If you can't find it at the local Radio Shack or electronics store, try Hello Direct, 800-444-3556. This is a catalog of devices, phones, headsets, and accessories for unusual telecommunications applications. The Web site address is: http://www.hello-direct.com.

To your clients and customers, their phone call or fax to your business must be a seamless, trouble-free event. Faxing, in particular, becomes a frustrating proposition in many make-do systems. If you're wondering if you can afford a business line, ask yourself this: Can I afford to have potential customers or clients feel that I am a rinky-dink operation? Your answer will most likely be an emphatic "no."

Special Telephone Services May Do the Job for You

Telecommunications services are evolving rapidly, and even more changes are coming with the passage of the Telecommunications Act. Here are some services available now that may meet your specific business needs:

- **Fax-back.** If your business depends on getting prices, specifications, pictures, schematics, or graphics into the hands of clients who call you, one option is an automatic fax-back capability, available either with programs for your PC or, if the volume warrants it, as separate, stand alone equipment. It works like this: A client (who must have a fax) calls a fax-back phone number promoted for the purpose. The system automatically sends the material back. The time-saving advantages are obvious, but if volume increases your phone line will be tied up a good part of the time.

- **E-mail-back.** Similar to fax-back, this will boot information back to people who query by e-mail, and store their message in your mailbox for further action. To respond with different kinds of information, use different addresses. Work with your Internet service provider to customize this feature.

- **PC-based answering systems.** Telephone answering systems for the PC offer several of the features mentioned above. Unless you want to leave your computer running all the time, however, you should look for one that has a "computer wake-up" feature that boots up the computer when the phone rings. Before you buy one of these, though, determine what impact the system will have on your daily work on the computer.

  Other features of these systems include voice messaging and fax-back. If extensive, automatic voice mail, fax-back, paging, and other features are a big part of your business, one option is to drag that old 386 out of the basement and set it up as a dedicated phone manager. You may have to upgrade it, and because these can be tricky to set up, plan to get your computer consultant involved. Still, PC-based phone systems are attractive to people who need to respond with sell sheets or catalogs, self-publishers, and those who do a lot of their work away from home base.

  Increasingly, a full range of telephone, fax, and paging features are being built into new computers and they include, in some cases, the ability to identify the calling number and pop the caller's file onto your screen before the phone is even answered.

- **Phantom phone number.** This is a phone number that lives in a computer operated by your basic phone service provider. There is no phone attached. It's like voice mail without being connected to a specific place such as your home or office. This is attractive to people who are on the move and want a permanent phone number, like sales reps. You also can operate multiple businesses with different names, each with its own phone number. It allows you to have multiple local phone numbers in cities anywhere, if that makes sense. You simply check for messages whenever you want, wherever you are.

- **800 and 888 numbers.** Toll-free numbers make you look big. Phone companies claim that customers are three to four times more willing to call a company for information if it has a toll-free number. Don't forget, you can use it yourself when traveling to check in with home base. It may actually be cheaper than using your calling card, depending on volume. The Federal Communications Commission created 888 numbers in 1996 because the country was running out of 800 numbers, but they are the same thing.

- **500 numbers.** Still new and not available everywhere, phone numbers with the 500 prefix are lifetime phone numbers, something like your Social Security number. If you love the idea of the ABC life (Always Being Connected), this could be for you. With a 500 number, phone calls will follow you whether at home, office, car, boat. Be aware that your client may get stuck with some surprising long-distance charges by dialing this number (unless you provide them with your PIN number). These 500 services are provided by AT&T (800-TRUE-500), MCI, Sprint, and others. The pricing is a little like cellular—expensive, but with optional programs that may suit your needs.

- **ISDN: The telecommunications hot rod.** A phone line setup that digitizes information and shoots it along in bursts, or packets, is being deployed across the country. Called ISDN, for Integrated Services Digital Network, it is currently used mostly by businesses who send large data files across long distances, or who want to connect their operations with teleconferencing facilities. But if you are deeply into an information-handling businesses, ISDN offers these three advantages:
    1. One line can do several tasks at once and replace multiple lines. You can simultaneously send and receive voice, data, images, and even video.

2. Sending data is very accurate and four times faster than today's fastest modems.
3. While it is more expensive than a business line, it is not outrageously more expensive on a monthly basis. Some additional hardware is also necessary, requiring what may add up to a few thousand dollars.

ISDN is the flavor of choice for people working in interactive multimedia because of the ability to send images, voice, and video. In addition to cost, the main obstacle is availability. For true ISDN you should be less than three miles from a phone company center because the signal degrades over distance, which means it is not available in rural areas except, perhaps, as Virtual ISDN. That's a conversation to have with your phone company if you're interested.

The Virtual Company

Our company has three partners who work from their homes located from five to 20 miles apart, and one associate in the Washington, D.C., area (who also spends a lot of time in the Middle East as a consultant). We all have Windows 95® and the same word processing program. This simple compatibility allows us to send fully formatted files back and forth.

Typically, we each draft "our" section of proposals and send them back and forth over the Internet for comment and criticism. The next improvement in our system will allow us to actually work on documents at the same time and see the changes on the computer monitor as they take place. This is done with personal conferencing software. With this type of software, people at computers at any locations can look at the same document and see each other's changes as they are made. It also shows the kind of small graphics normally found in documents. This can be a big asset for partners like us, and for businesses such as law firms or advertising agencies who need to share draft copies of material immediately. It also can connect a "home base" to remote job sites. The software can be used over a Local Area Network and upgraded to add PC-based video conferencing.

This virtual office capability is just emerging, but promises to be a technology like the fax machine: One day you never heard of it, the next day everybody has to have it. Personal conferencing is made to order for telecommuting and partnering.

CHAPTER 10

Preparing for and Surviving Rainy Days

"If you're being chased by a crocodile, run in a zigzag pattern because they can only run fast on a straightaway."

—Father Guido Sarducci (Don Novello)

*I*f you have not been paying attention to your day-to-day marketing, you can hit a dry spell that can push you to your financial limits. Having gone through the recession of the early 1990s and a few very fat periods that made me lazy about marketing, I speak from experience. All my hubris has been rendered out by dry spells.

You also may come to a point at which you choose to seek greener pastures, either because you are looking for a better economic climate or because you want to head for the country life and join the "lone eagles" who live and work off the beaten track.

Let's take a look at some options for preparing for rainy days, surviving them, and choosing a new location.

Setbacks versus Catastrophes

The setback. If you have been on your own for a couple of years, you may have hit your first dry spell and thought it was a catastrophe. It is likely (and perhaps inevitable) that you will be severely *underemployed* for a period of time for all the reasons described earlier. It is not unusual for this to become a cycle connected to getting lazy about marketing. The frightening part is: You don't know how long a setback will last. What you can be sure of, however, is that even when your luck turns around it can be 30, 60, or 90 days before the working/billing cycle puts an adequate supply of money into the till.

If you haven't hit a setback, prepare for one while times are good. Set up a revolving "setback" fund. For setbacks, three to six months' worth of income is realistic. If you're not sure about what you would actually need, complete the worksheet for analyzing your financial situation in the appendix of this book.

When times are good, keep rebuilding the fund with regular contributions. Before April 15 of each year, when you are doing your taxes, evaluate the amount in the fund. If it is larger than it needs to be, contribute to a SEP-IRA or similar plan with as much as you can to avoid paying taxes on the money.

Without the emergency cushion, you may have to rely more, but prudently, on credit cards, lines of credit, home equity loans, and other means of bridging the gap.

The catastrophe. In a real catastrophe, that three-to-six-month fund will evaporate long before the problem is over. Surveys show that about a third of all self-employed people rely on a spouse's health insurance, but about 14 percent don't have any. It stretches the tolerance for risk discussed in Chapter 7 to an extreme limit.

You will have to come to grips with severe cutbacks in the way you spend and deal with debt, make special arrangements with lenders, and make use of government safety net programs. If you have become overextended on credit and are facing aggressive collection techniques, get in touch with the consumer protection agency in your area to understand your rights and options.

A permanent collapse in business can mean your sanity test was not accurate, conditions have changed, and it's time to consider other options, such as relocating. A noted small business columnist recently wrote that she vowed to start looking for a job if she had to borrow against her home to support the business. It depends on your tolerance for risk. But I have had friends go bankrupt after pouring everything they owned and as much as 30 years into a losing proposition.

Moonlighting as a "Temp"

Each working day, more than two million people head off to temporary jobs. It is one of the fastest-growing segments of the work force. Once upon a time a temporary employee was someone you got through an agency when the regular receptionist was on vacation, or you had a pile of typing to do that no one could handle. No more. Today's temporary employee is more frequently a freelance professional with skills in computers, programming, health care, management, accounting, marketing, and even law. Here are several circumstances that make temporary employment an option worth considering:

- When you need to moonlight to tide you over the setback or catastrophe. The need for additional income is the number one reason people turn to temporary employment, as cited by 78 percent of the workers surveyed for the National Association of Temporary and Staffing Services (NAISS).
- When you want to get back into the work force and hope the temporary position will lead to a full-time job. In fact, nearly 40 percent of the temporary workers surveyed were asked if they wanted to work full-time.
- When you're interested in a new career field and want to experience it firsthand before making a big commitment. You may find a temporary position that allows you to test drive a career change.
- When you want some new training and experience to brush up on old skills or learn new ones. Temporary services are

frequently involved in training, and nearly half of the temporary workers surveyed had received free training.
- When personal or family commitments are such that you simply can't work for yourself or anyone else full-time, but want to keep active in your field of work.
- When you like the idea of working only when you want to. Of the workers who were asked to work full-time, 38 percent declined and opted to continue on as freelancers.

The universe of temporary or contract employees has been growing at about 12 percent per year (although for a few years it was greater than 20 percent) since the beginning of the decade, faster than the overall growth in the work-at-home movement. In the decade from 1985 to 1995, the "temp" work force went from 0.68 percent of the total work force to 1.78 percent, and the *Washington Post* reported that temporary work is responsible for 8 percent of the new job growth since 1993.

The vast majority of temporary workers are still women working in so-called "pink-collar jobs"—clerical or administrative support. But the percentage of men is increasing and approaching 30 percent. The shifts have come in two growth areas: white-collar workers in technical areas, health care, professions, and marketing, and blue-collar labor.

About Pay and Benefits

The temporary employee will rarely receive pay and benefits comparable to the full-time employee at the next work station. Overall, the average temporary worker makes between $9 and $10 an hour, but the managers and professionals who make up about 10 percent of the temporary work force earn anywhere from $15 to $75 an hour.

One fact to bear in mind is that as a temporary you work *at* a variety of different businesses, but you work *for* the temporary service you choose. Shop around. If you are using temp work to carry you through an emergency and have your own benefits under control, the service is not a big issue. If, however, you decide on a life as a career "temp," benefits do exist in the form of training, paid holidays, bonuses, and, to a lesser extent, health care, life insurance, sick pay, and retirement plans. Health insurance is the crunch for everyone now, and even if it is available it may be out of reach because of the cost of your share. Your accountant also can advise you on the impact on deductions for any equipment you've already purchased, or the home office deduction.

Working as a temporary employee is not for everyone. Perhaps the two most valuable traits are flexibility and a willingness to learn. Temps are able to choose their hours, their days, their vacations, and their assignments, but they also will have to

- step into new companies in new work environments and be ready to perform,
- adapt to equipment, materials, or formats that may be unfamiliar,
- learn to fit into a company's individual way of doing things, even if it doesn't seem to make much sense, and
- take assignments on very short notice.

Although you may tend to think of temporary service positions as being just a day or two long, 45 percent of the individuals surveyed for NATSS had assignments averaging five to 26 weeks.

Moving to Greener Pastures

Some people strike out on their own because their company job has moved, and if they want to continue working they have to relocate. That's why I left corporate life. But for some folks the opposite is true, they want to move: They want to flee dangerous cities and enjoy the sense of safety and community provided by small town life. Some are empty nesters, ready to move to a smaller home or condo with less maintenance in a better climate. For others, declining economic conditions make a move necessary.

For whatever reasons, there has been a long, continuous migration from the cities to rural areas beyond the suburbs. The trend is so pervasive that trend watcher Gerald Celente of the Trends Research Institute has identified "technotribalism"—the creation of new post-industrial communities in rural areas—as one of the major forces in the new millennium. Phil Burgess, president of the Center for the New West, has coined the term "lone eagles" for the growing number of freelance professionals who, through technology, can now work where they live and live wherever they wish.

Are you planted in fertile ground for your business? Do you want to start over in a place where quality of life, safety, a sense of community, and small town values dominate the horizon? Can you have both? Probably. Will you make as much money? Probably not, but maybe. The question is: What's most important to you?

Let's consider some criteria for deciding if moving you and your business is right for you. These are not factors you will want to add up in columns and use to try to come to some absolute truth based on the numbers, but they are essential. The two important things to remember are:

1. **Don't set yourself up to fail.**
2. **"Because I want to . . ." is a perfectly good reason,** as long as you understand the costs. These costs do not always have to do with money.

Consideration #1: Being Near the Money

As the story goes, Willie Sutton was a bank robber who had not been entirely successful. Arrested again, a cop asked, "Willie, why do you keep on robbing banks?"

"Because," said Willie, "that's where the money is."

It is a good idea to be close to your source of income. Being near Fortune 500 companies is nice, if you plan to subcontract to them. Government power centers are good. The question is: Can faxes, overnight delivery services, networking, and the like do an adequate job of getting new clients as well as serving existing clients? Small rural areas rarely have the business infrastructure to provide an adequate base for a service business. Your clients will be elsewhere. Our small community has a consultant's network. A survey of the members showed that those who did most of their business locally made less than $30,000 a year. Those who did most of their business outside the state made over $75,000 and, in a few cases, $100,000. There was almost nobody in the middle of the $30,000 to $75,000 range. Work locally and starve or work nationally and prosper was the message from the survey.

If "technotribalism" operates as projected, many corporate headquarters will follow the migration to rural areas for quality of life considerations. However, even if you settle in a small town that has its own version of Microsoft, you must think about having all your eggs in that particular basket.

And when it comes to shoring up business relationships, it is hard to beat a good lunch. You don't have to be with your clients in person all the time, but you will need to be there when you are trying to get the new business and when you are trying to keep it from being stolen by someone who can provide more service in person. So, an alternative to being near the money all the time is being near a darned good airport, and being prepared to consider airfare in the cost of your freedom.

Consideration #2: Affordability

What will it cost to move the business? For many home offices, it's a matter of packing up the computer and supplies and loading them on the truck with everything else. You will have to print new letterhead and marketing materials and notify your clients of the change. Losing clients is the greatest risk.

One of the biggest factors will be housing, and moving from a suburban metropolitan area to a small, more rural community can be a wonderful surprise when it comes to housing costs. City auto insurance rates are usually much higher than small town rates. But as a home-based business here are other considerations that translate into costs or benefits:

- Is there a personal income tax?
- Are utility costs reasonable? Factor in the climate.
- If you are a heavy user of online information services, is there a local Internet service provider with a local phone number or will you pay long-distance charges while online?
- Is this a starving community where everything government does shows up in your real estate taxes? School taxes are usually the biggest chunk. They vary from town to town, and reflect the amount of industry that helps pay the tax

bills. With an IBM factory in town, the best schools and lowest taxes go hand in hand.
- Is this community growing or shrinking? How much will you pay for infrastructure growth (like schools)? Will your investment in your home grow or shrink?
- Is there a Health Maintenance Organization (HMO) in the area? The HMO is often the best (and least expensive) choice for health coverage, but not every small town has one.

Consideration #3: Business Climate

Some regions of the country are booming, but others have been struggling to find a new engine of growth since the recession. The economy is flat. Those of us in service businesses yearn for the old days when manufacturing was an economic force and somebody was actually putting tops on bottoms and not just moving information around. Here are some other factors to consider:

- Is there a market for your business nearby? Does there need to be?
- The combined tax picture.
- Is the community friendly or restrictive in terms of zoning and small business permits?
- A healthy downtown business district is a good sign, but retailers don't buy much from consultants and service providers unless you have a specialty product or useful service for them.
- Colleges and universities add a wonderful dimension of intellectual and cultural activity to a community, but also may be a source of competition for certain kinds of consulting. My partners and I routinely compete with faculty members who run sideline businesses from their university offices, which we help to subsidize through taxes.
- Does the work force have a supply of competent people to help you do your books, prepare your taxes, consult on financial matters, fix your computer, help you unravel the mysteries of your new software, and partner with you on large jobs?

- Does the transportation system, particularly the airport, meet your requirements for travel?
- Can you do business with the local banks? A commercial banker can be a great source of information about a community.
- Is this area served by Federal Express, Airborne Express, UPS, or another overnight courier service? Can you conduct your business without one?

Consideration #4: Quality of Life

Good schools, access to recreation, cultural events, scenery, safety, a sense of community, and other such factors have an enormous influence on how well you live. There are other factors mentioned less often but that are equally important:

- Who will be your friends, and the kids' friends?
- Does the local culture work for you? Can you substitute a rodeo for the ballet, or simple living for access to shopping?
- Can you stand the climate? Try a visit during the off-season. Phoenix in August, Burlington, Vermont, early in February. Falling in love with a New England community on a July evening, with silky breezes blowing across the meadow windflowers, is not the same as waking up every morning for a week with the temperature at 17 degrees below zero.

Scoping Out a Community

If you have your eye on a community and want to test drive it, start with the local chamber of commerce or industrial development group. They will happily send you a package of basic information. Just don't expect them to go out of their way to say anything critical about their communities. If the community is too small for such organizations, start at the state level with the travel and tourism or industrial development departments. Spending a few minutes dialing 1-(area code)-555-1212 should turn up an organization. The more aggressive states and communities will have a home page on the Internet.

SUREFIRE TIP

Subscribe. To really get a feel for the fabric of a community, subscribe to the local daily (or weekly) newspaper for three months. Don't forget to read the classified ads, because you will learn a lot about real estate prices and job opportunities. You also will learn about crime, schools, culture, recreation, and the weather. For about $30, you can virtually move into any community you choose for three months.

An excellent book on the topic of relocating is *Country Bound! Trade Your Business Suit Blues for Blue Jean Dreams* by Marilyn and Tom Ross. The authors practice what they preach: They operate three national businesses from a town of 2,000 nestled between 14,000-foot Colorado mountains. Their book overflows with practical advice about rural relocation and running a successful business in the boonies. If you can't find it in your book store, order it direct for $19.95 plus $5 shipping by calling 800-829-7934 for credit card orders or fax 312-836-1021, Attention EMJ. Checks can be sent to Dearborn Financial Publishing, Inc., Dept. EMJ, 155 North Wacker Drive, Chicago, IL 60606-1719.

A Few Good Cities

Every year, *Home Office Computing* magazine selects the top ten cities for home-based businesses based on factors like those mentioned previously. The magazine's site on the Internet is a good place to look for its latest choices: http://www.small-office.com. Gaithersburg, Maryland, made the list for three years, but here are some other top choices:

- Phoenix, Arizona
- Austin, Texas
- Pittsburgh, Pennsylvania
- Kansas City, Missouri
- Seattle, Washington

10 / Preparing for and Surviving Rainy Days

- Portland, Oregon
- Minneapolis-St. Paul, Minnesota
- Lincoln, Nebraska
- Columbia, South Carolina
- Atlanta, Georgia
- Provo, Utah
- St. Peters, Missouri
- Burlington, Vermont
- St. Petersburg, Florida
- Aurora, Colorado

Others who have ranked cities on quality of life, but not necessarily a favorable climate for lone eagles, have singled out:

- Bozeman, Montana
- Columbia, Missouri
- Durango, Colorado
- Eugene, Oregon
- Fayetteville, Arkansas
- Gettysburg, Pennsylvania
- Madison, Wisconsin
- Olympia, Washington
- Waco, Texas

CHAPTER 11

Working from Anywhere
The Mobile Office

> *"Work anywhere, anytime is the new paradigm. Your car, your home, your office, even your client's office. Work alone, coupled, teamed. Work in real space or in cyberspace. It amounts to a massive disaggregation of work, spinning outside the walls and confines of the traditional office."*
> —Business Week *cover story on "The New Workplace"*

One of the consequences of growth and success—or moving to the country—is that home business owners spend more time working with widely-scattered clients and less time at home. Your range of operations can quickly expand from around the corner to across the country. From my little home office in Vermont I have packed up my notebook computer and headed off to work for days and even weeks at a time in Manhattan, California, and South Carolina. My partners worked for a week in Argentina, and we are currently writing a proposal for work in California, Europe, and Hong Kong. Consequently, we, like other home-based businesses, increasingly have to be everywhere at once, and be able to communicate with clients and home from almost anywhere.

The trend toward working on the road has become so widespread that it has produced two new terms, the "road warrior" and "hoteling." A few large companies are pioneering hoteling. They have done away with individual permanent offices for the "road warriors" on their sales and customer service staffs, but provide office spaces in strategic locations where the mobile work force can conduct meetings, plug in notebook computers, use phones, work, and connect to the company's communications network. These spaces can be reserved through a facilities manager or concierge, who also may arrange to have files and other necessary items forwarded in advance for meetings.

SUREFIRE TIP

How to be there when you're not there. There *is* a way to get your mail and accept UPS, FedEx, and similar deliveries even when nobody is home. Mail Boxes Etc. will rent you a post office box (it can be your business address if you need to separate home and work activities) that comes bundled with several handy services. They will accept parcels for you and notify you, forward your mail if necessary, and provide 24-hour access to your mail box. Plus, you have 24-hour access for copying if you get a prepaid copy card. Mail Boxes Etc. also can give you your own fax number, and call you when a fax comes in. Mail Boxes Etc. has 2,000 locations in the United States, Canada, and internationally. And, of course, they carry office supplies and handle shipping chores.

Mobile technology can provide e-mail and all the other communications tools no matter where you are, but there are caveats:

- One problem is deciding which option is best at a time when mobile communication is one of the most rapidly-changing areas of technology. So, I'll focus on where you will be able to find the most current information on products and services, not on the products and services themselves. Additional Internet sources of mobile information are listed in Appendix B.
- Big cities have mobile communications specialists, but in the rest of the country it can be tough to find anyone who

really knows what they are talking about to get you up and running.
- And, finally, state-of-the-art mobile technology often comes up short in reliability or affordability.

The choices fall into these general categories:

- Notebook computers, mobile printers, computer/cellular phone connections
- Pagers, which also offer e-mail access
- Personal digital assistants (PDAs)—miniature computerlike devices with communications features
- The newest option, PCS (Personal Communications Services)

Notebook Computers and Portable Printers for the Mobile Worker

A first step toward the mobile office is the notebook computer and portable computer printer. Notebook computers are reviewed and compared every month in magazines like *Mobile Office, PC World,* and *Home Office Computing.* Your task is to decide how many features you need in a notebook.

Portable printers are not found in most retail stores unless it is a store that caters to the mobile worker. But small battery-operated portables do exist. Some are very small, smaller than a carton of cigarettes. Others are very high quality and color printers, but these are larger. Here's a few companies you can call for information on portable printers:

- Canon Computer Systems, 800-848-4123; Internet: *http://www.usa.canon.com*
- Citizen America Corp., 800-477-4683; Internet: *http://www.citizen-america.com*
- Hewlett-Packard, 800-752-0900; Internet: *http://www.hp.com*
- Mannesmann Tally Corp., 1-206-251-5500; Internet: *http://www.tally.com*
- Pentax Technologies, 800-543-6144; Internet: *http://pentaxtech.com*

As Simple as ABC—Always Being Connected

The next step is connecting a regular land line or cellular phone to your notebook to turn it into a communications device for sending and receiving e-mail, files, and faxes, just like the big computer back home. You can plug into a regular phone line just about anywhere.

If you must send and receive large amounts of data such as contracts, proposals, detailed messages, and so on, take advantage of the fact that your online information service (CompuServe, America Online, MSN, Prodigy, etc.) probably has a local telephone number you can dial into from wherever you are. Your Internet service provider may or may not have a local number. Major long-distance providers like AT&T, MCI, and Sprint who serve as links to the Internet usually have local access numbers across the country.

SUREFIRE TIP

A monthly magazine, *Mobile Office* is devoted entirely to portable technology. A particularly handy reference is its monthly *Mobile Market Roundup,* a digest of hardware and software reviews about products the magazine has tested. It includes concise comments on the products and identifies the top-rated product. For subscription information, call: 800-274-1218. For latest mobile news, articles and hot links to about 200 sites related to mobile offices visit their web site at *http://www.mobileoffice.com/*.

If you're in your hotel, talk to the concierge about getting online through their business services. Some people carry an acoustic coupler that simply fits on a telephone handset to allow you to hook up the computer. Many communities now have cyber cafes, where you can get an espresso while connecting. Be sure you know your necessary passwords and codes.

The Notebook Computer and Cellular Phone Hookup

It is fairly simple to connect a cellular phone to a notebook computer to be able to send and receive faxes and e-mail if you need to, but you will pay for computer-cellular connecting devices and for high per-minute cellular rates. You also may encounter technology quirks that make it necessary to make a couple of tries before you get complete messages.

The area of wireless communications is moving so fast that the latest and best information is often available from the web sites of your local service provider, which is a Baby Bell or one of its competitors who provide dial tone. For the national view, try these Internet sites:

- MCI is at *http://www.mci.com*. Phone: 800-246-5610.
- AT&T is at *http://www.attws.com*. Phone: 800-426-2229.
- Sprint is at *http://www.sprint.com*. Phone: 800-877-2000.

SUREFIRE TIP

Stretch notebook use with a power inverter. The battery in an automobile, boat, car, or recreation vehicle can be used to power your notebook computer with a power inverter. This is a little black box that accepts the three-pronged plug of your notebook's battery charger. It has a short cord with a cigarette lighter plug on the end. The job of the inverter is to change DC battery power to AC power, like house power. The small ones, capable of handling a notebook computer, cost around $50. Of course, you have to take with you the notebook's black box for plugging into house power, but it gives you the longer life of a big 12-volt auto battery and allows you to recharge your notebook battery, too. Look for inverters at electronics and marine supply stores, or in catalogs from those places. Catalogers like Damart also carry them.

Pagers Challenge Cellular Capabilities

If you still hold the old notion that paging is an archaic system for doctors on call, a second look at today's pagers is a real surprise. They offer features that suit some people's needs better than cellular phones—e-mail, for example—and new features are constantly becoming available.

Like cellular phones, you subscribe to a carrier and can choose from local paging services and national services that offer wide coverage and premium services at higher prices. Also like cellular, you may (or may not) have to key in your intention to roam.

You may own or lease the pager. If you buy one at a national chain such as Service Merchandise, Staples, CompUSA, and Target, you will be signing on with one of the national services like those listed below. The four nationwide leaders in the pager field are:

1. PageNet, the world's largest nationwide service, with voice paging. Phone: 800-724-3638.
2. MobileComm, second largest. Phone: 800-234-6542.
3. Sky-Tel, with nationwide two-way paging and premium services. Phone: 800-759-6058.
4. PageMart, fastest growing. Phone: 800-324-PAGE.

The major long-distance providers, whose numbers were listed earlier in the chapter, also offer paging services.

SUREFIRE TIP

Some cellular owners use a paging service to make sure they are aware of all attempts to reach them and then make a decision on which ones need a call back immediately from the cellular. This cuts down on high per-minute cellular costs and can be a good option for "on call" businesses like computer repair.

Personal Digital Assistants Become Communicators

At first glance, a personal digital assistant looks like a computer wannabe—a tiny little keyboard too small for use by anyone larger than a munchkin. The PDA has more appeal to a road warrior (e.g., sales representative, insurance agent, troubleshooting consultant) than to a writer or designer, but low cost and increasingly useful communication functions are creating a new niche for PDAs as portable devices that can talk to the big computer back home. They received a big boost with the introduction of Microsoft Windows CE, a PDA software package that resembles Windows 95® and contains small versions of Word, Excel, and Internet Explorer. This not only gives the PDA software a familiar feel for Microsoft users, it makes it easy to swap files between the little unit and the desktop back home.

The PDA's ability to communicate is accomplished both by including fax modems for connection to normal telephone land lines, and by marrying them to paging systems or cellular phones.

This market has attracted some serious competitors, including Apple (Newton), Casio, Hewlett-Packard, Motorola, Sharp, and Sony. PDAs are widely available in office supply, electronics, and discount stores.

Different models of PDAs tend to be strong in one area at the expense of other features. Some are superb communicators, some offer better handwriting recognition than others, some are strong organizing and contact management tools and offer lots of software applications. If you are in the market, shop carefully so you don't pay for features you don't need (pen writing, for example) and get the features you do need (the ability to link to your home computer, if that's one).

You can pick and choose from these features offered by different models and manufacturers:

- Built-in fax modems for connection to land lines
- Connectivity to your home computer, via serial or infrared ports
- Printer connectivity
- PC card slots, for adding fax modem cards for cellular, land line, or radio communication

- Connectivity to paging, data messages, and stock quotes through links like PageNet StarLink
- Bundled software like Microsoft Works, Lotus 1-2-3, cc: Mail Remote, Pocket Quicken, and, for the Newton, an abundance of software and shareware that includes applications for specific occupations and professions
- Built-in software to connect you to your online information service, like CompuServe. Hooked into a telephone line, you can send and receive your e-mail and access other services offered by your online service.

PDAs often have a preferred communications service, so that is another factor to consider when you go shopping for a PDA. You already may be on one service and don't need to get started with another one. These are links such as eWorld, CompuServe, AOL, PageNet StarLink, AT&T PersonalLink, RadioMail, and ARDIS.

Personal Communications Services

PCS, or personal communications services, are 100 percent digital cellular communicators, able to handle voice, data, and video communication from almost anywhere, anytime. A typical product is a single telephone number that reaches your combination cellular phone, pager, and voice mail. The advantages are better (digital) quality, more features, smaller phones and other devices, longer battery life, the potential for greater privacy and security, and possibly lower prices.

To get the latest on PCS, here are some contacts. These Web sites have the latest new product press releases from their sponsors:

- AT&T Wireless, phone 888-299-8558 or go to their Web page at *http://www.airdata.com.*
- MCI is at *http://www.mci.com.* Phone: 800-246-5610.
- Sprint, call 800-480-4PCS, or go to the Web site at *http://www.sprintpcs.com.*

For the Road

Communicating from the road often boils down to a matter of details. Before heading out, ask yourself:

- Wherever I am, do I know how to find the local phone number for my online information service or Internet service provider? Keep the provider's customer service number handy.
- Do I know all the passwords and codes necessary to establish my connection?
- If I have to, do I know how to configure my modem without having manuals available? You can always copy the necessary instructions.
- Do I have a supply of necessary "goes-intas," the all-important jacks and connectors that allow me to put everything together?

CHAPTER 12

The Outlook for Working from Home

*"All men should strive to learn before they die
What they are running from, and to, and why."*
—James Thurber

*I*n 1980, the year people were beginning to hear about things called personal computers, Alvin Toffler's book *The Third Wave* predicted obsolete assembly lines and the rise of home-based businesses in "a novel institution that might be called 'the electronic cottage.'" He predicted the trend involved decentralization and deurbanization of production, and would return millions of people to their homes as a workplace.

Today, about a million people per year are added to the ranks of the full-time, self-employed work-at-home, and millions more work for corporations but spend all or part of their work week "telecommuting" from home offices.

Futurist Faith Popcorn has suggested that by 2010 all the brightest and best people will have left corporations and will be working from home, communicating electronically. Joel Barker of Infinity, Limited, has constructed a set of implications for the growth of the "electronic cottage" that point toward excess office space, less urban sprawl, reduced travel, growth in the electronics industry, and more family interaction.

Gerald Celente, founder of the Trends Research Institute in Rhinebeck, New York, and author of "Trends 2000: How to Prepare For and Profit from the Changes of the 21st Century" (Warner Books), points to a major trend he calls "technotribalism." It is a melding of corporate downsizing, economic fallback, the home office trend, interactive communications, and a big push to small towns. Corporate headquarters follow workers to rural areas, the home office becomes a room designed into new homes like the kitchen and bathrooms, and a movement toward home education rattles the education institutions. Not everyone can work from home, of course, but working from home ceases to be the curiosity it became in the early 1990s.

Or is this just a passing fad that has been highly hyped and will never live up to expectations?

I asked some of the people who have been following this movement to comment on where they see the home work trend in ten years.

The Futurist's View: Glen Hiemstra

Glen Hiemstra is a professional speaker, consulting futurist, and author who lives near Redmond, Washington. He is coauthor of *Strategic Leadership: Achieving Your Preferred Future* and of *Leadership Library 1.0*. His Web site is: *www.futurist.com*.

The last time a century turned, in 1900, only 13 percent of the American work force had "jobs." By 1977, 93 percent of the American work force had jobs, which had come to mean working for an organization, doing specified work at a specified time each day, in exchange for a salary and health and retirement benefits. All of this gave the job holder "security." Then the world changed.

Now, faster than all but a few imagine, a confluence of social, economic, but most of all technological forces are bringing a new world of work, in which each person is a "business of one." Most people still work for organizations, but by the second decade of the 21st Century those who hold a stable job with salary and benefits will be the minority. Others will work in organizations, but in something that may be better labeled a "stint" than a "job." A growing number will work as individuals. In fact the information revolution is liberating individuals as never before.

Three key technologies will create opportunity and challenge for the home-based or individual worker in the next ten years. Commerce on the Net is first. The basic home computer in 2007 will have enormous RAM and storage capacity. Into this box will come a big pipe capable of data transmission at 28 million bits a second. From the box pipes will go to many screens in the home, essentially wherever you have a screen or phone in 1997. Each screen will have a variety of pointing, clicking, speaking, or typing devices, and all will be connected to the worldwide Net. And that Net will bring into your home an astonishing array of both learning and commercial opportunities, many of them in full two-way video toward the end of the ten-year horizon.

For the first time in history anyone can sell into and buy from a global market. Individuals of imagination and ambition will join this cybereconomy and discover that the greatest source of wealth will be the ideas in your head rather than physical capital alone.

The second technology is that combination of factors leading to a rapidly increasing lifespan, and implications for retirement. Retirement is based on the notion that after age 65 you will live the rest of your life on accumulated savings and benefits. But when this system was invented, it was assumed that the average person would live only three or four years after retirement. The human lifespan has nearly tripled in the past 200 years, from an average of 35 years to nearly 80 years. If you reach 65 and are healthy, you can anticipate living another 20 years. There are prospects that this could jump dramatically in the early 21st Century particularly due to genetic engineering. The implications are clear for the home-based, individual worker. Start redefining now how you will live after age 65.

The final technology is a soft rather than hard one, and not so new at that. It will be those technologies of goal setting, self-management, and achieving balance which will become more and more critical in a world which leaves individuals far more responsible for themselves than people grew accustomed to in the 20th Century world of industry. When you are a "business of one" there is no time clock to tell you when to stop working, no human resources department to manage your benefits, and no manager to tell you it is time for advancement or change. There is only you. This change is liberating, but also unsettling and even frightening. Managing yourself in a world of uncertainty, opportunity, and rapid change will be the greatest challenge of the next ten years.

The Researcher's View: Raymond Boggs, IDC/Link

Raymond Boggs is director of the Home Office Research Program for IDC/Link, a market research firm with offices in New York City and Framingham, Massachusetts. IDC/Link has conducted annual surveys on home office and telecommuting trends since 1989. You can access their Web site at *www.idcresearch.com*.

The overall growth rate of all types of home workers—self-employed, telecommuters, part-time self-employed and those who bring work home from the office—has been from 8 to 10 percent a year since the late 1980s. It has topped 30 million households, and it is conceivable that at the turn of the century about a quarter of the work force will be working full- or part-time from home.

The percentage of growth has to decline somewhat simply because the base is getting larger and larger, but the growth in numbers continues. We're adding about a million people a year to the ranks of the full-time self-employed home worker. Some are dropping out—the rate could be from 4 to 6 percent—but the number of new people coming in produces a significant net increase

We expect that the number of full-time self-employed will stabilize at fewer than one in five workers. An important factor in home-worker success is how committed people are to running a home-based business. If you were caught by surprise in a company downsizing and starting a home business was just one option, along with calling a headhunter and all your friends to find a new job, your home business is doomed from the start. If you're just going into it for the money, you're also in trouble. But if you have always been interested in running a home-based business, if you have lined up finances, and if you also have done a business plan, then you are on the right path. The successful home entrepreneur needs passion, commitment, and almost evangelical fervor. You can see it in focus groups; people just love to talk about their home business. They need a high resilience to adversity, because setbacks are inevitable and failure can become self-fulfilling. Optimism is a key commodity for home-based businesses. You have to believe you can be up to bat ten times and strike out, and still know that on the next pitch you'll hit a home run. Really enjoying the work is also important, although many complain about the long hours. Effective home workers are often satisfied, even delighted, by the quality and nature of their work, although no one else may seem to appreciate it.

The nature of working from home is also changing. Corporate home workers are getting more and more support from their companies. The same downsizing pressures that are feeding the spread of home-based businesses are encouraging corporate home working. After all, not all the work can be outsourced! Those remaining on staff now have more to do than ever. As part of expanding the workday we've had to expand the workplace. People now work everywhere, to squeeze out every productive minute—while commuting, while flying, even while walking. We are all becoming mobile workers.

The Future of Telecommuting: Gil Gordon, Consultant

Gil Gordon is a consultant and expert on telecommuting. He publishes a newsletter on the topic and organizes an annual telecommuting conference. He has helped design telecommuting programs for some of America's largest companies, and is coauthor of *Telecommuting—How to Make It Work for You and Your Company*. You can reach him at his Web site at *www.gilgordon.com*.

What will telecommuting be like in ten years? For starters, I'm hoping that the word will disappear from the language—at least in terms of how we use it today. This will be a sign that the concept is fully integrated into the work world, even if everyone doesn't do it.

Let me explain: When telephones first came into the office around the turn of the century, the activity called "telephoning" was quite novel, and people could be classified as "telephoners" and "non-telephoners" depending on whether they had one of those scarce instruments on their desk. Today, of course, those terms are laughable—phones are everywhere, and if we need to make or take a call, we use them. I'm looking forward to the time when "telecommuting" and "telecommuters" similarly fade into the background.

I'm also hopeful that the relatively few remaining technical glitches that prevent seamless, simple, reliable telecommuting in all cases will have gone away. Telecommuting has never been held back seriously by the lack of technology; even today, we have more than we know what to do with. But the problem is that the more we have, the more we want—and we seem to have reached a plateau of sorts. In particular, the weak leg of the hardware-software-telecommunications stool is the last one; despite tremendous advances in telecommunications technology, it remains the source of much frustration for managers and employers trying to implement advanced telecommuting solutions.

Last, I believe the success and effect of telecommuting will be most visible in the size, form, and design of offices and office buildings. Yes, we'll still have offices—I don't for a minute believe they will, or should, all disappear. But they will look different and be used differently, and will become just ONE place to work and not THE place to work. The average number of square feet of personal space per worker will continue to decline, and more space will be devoted to various kinds of group and team interaction areas. The office of ten years from now will likely be a weird combination of an airline's airport club room, a Starbuck's coffee shop, a library, and a Kinko's store—multiple functions, multiple activity areas, various kinds of individual and group work areas, and lots of support services close at hand.

Most important, ten years from now I'll be doing something entirely different. I've been involved in the telecommuting field since 1982, and a 25-year run is much more than I bargained for. It's been great fun while it lasted, however!

For "Stats" Fans: Research Profiles the Home Worker

Research firms differ somewhat on how many people work at least part time from home, with the numbers ranging from 41 to 47 million individuals, or 30 to 39 million households. The growth rate is about 8 to 10 percent a year *(IDC/Link Resources)*. The estimates of those who are earning their primary income as self-employed home workers ranges from 13 to 18 million. The small business administration says there are 16 million part- and full-time self-employed individuals. There are estimated to be 3.5 million home-based businesses operated by self-employed women, providing full- or part-time employment for about 14 million people *(National Foundation for Women Business Owners)*.

Profiled by Find/SVP Research, 55 percent of home workers are male, typical age of 40, with an average household income of $54,300. Professional services such as consultants, lawyers, editors, researchers, teachers, and technical skills, account for 53 percent.

A survey conducted by the American Association of Home-Based Businesses and Canon USA shows home workers work fewer hours (33.6 per week) but work more evenings and weekends. They don't miss: the daily commute (26%), the overbearing boss (21%), and the set business hours (14%). They do miss: company benefits (26%), interaction with fellow workers (25%), and financial security (23%).

Sales of services and products for home offices have topped $14 billion *(IDC/Link)*, with 44 percent of all U.S. households having an income-generating home office *(BIS Strategic Decisions)*. About 60 percent of all home offices have a computer *(School & Home Office Products Association)*. Some 6 million households have a telecommuter inside, and another 10 million have a home office used for bringing work home from the company office *(IDC/Link)*.

A reader survey by *Home Office Computing* magazine says the top reason for starting a home business was "got fed up with corporate life," with the second spot going to "got laid off/downsized from a corporate job." Eighty-eight percent had worked in a corporate environment. A desire to spend more time with family was among the top five reasons for starting a home business on all surveys.

And, as for you, welcome to the technotribe.

APPENDIX A

Useful Internet Addresses

The Internet is rapidly becoming something I can't fully fathom at this point. I have found some parts of it very valuable for researching topics and businesses, some parts of it moderately enjoyable for checking out my own pet interests and communicating with others who share them, and some parts similar to citizens band radio at its heyday, when so many people were talking and so few were saying anything worth hearing. It also can waste a lot of valuable time by tempting users—especially home business people working alone—to get distracted and wander around in cyberspace.

Little by little, however, I've warmed up to the World Wide Web. More often than not I can find what I need to know faster on the Web than by calling an 800 number and being shuffled through voice mail and finally landing back where I started, none the wiser.

Expanding Domains

For most of the Web's history, the most commonly used "domains" (the little tag after the dot following the main address) have been:

- For businesses: .com
- For organizations: .org

161

- For educational institutions: .edu
- For government: .gov

These domains are supplemented by some new ones:

- For businesses: .firm
- For electronic storefronts: .store
- For cultural and entertainment sites: .arts
- For information services: .info
- For individuals with personal sites: .nom
- For recreational activities: .rec
- For entitites emphasizing the World Wide Web: .web

I know of only one Web site that will give me exactly what I want every time I hit it: The U.S. Naval Observatory Clock Web site always gives the exact time (or close enough, maybe it takes a few nanoseconds for the information to travel from the clock to my monitor). It will also tell me how my computer's internal clock compares to correct time. The site is at: *http://tycho.usno.navy.mil/what.html.*

http://www

Many sites on the Web are both interesting and helpful to home-based businesses. Here are some I visit periodically to see what's new or to conduct research. I have dropped the ***http://www*** prefix from the addresses listed in italics in the following sections to cut down on repetition. Many of these sites are hot-linked to dozens of related topics, so they are good starting points for exploring.

Topic: Self-Employment, Working from Home

aboutwork.com   This is a very chatty Web page, both in its breezy style and graphics and in the fact it has frequent chat sessions and daily polls of its visitors. At first it is a little confusing to navigate, but its basic topic areas are Jobs, Career Planning, Work from Home, Start-up Dreams, and a Resource Center. It also has several chat areas: Chat, Feedback, Discussion Groups, Bitch and Moan. If you're lonely, angry, or looking for advice on specific topics, give it a try. For all its funky style, I downloaded a fill-in-the-blanks model business plan that was a serious package for a small business getting ready to go a bank for financing.

bradyrooms.com   This company makes sunrooms, but has taken the idea of a modular addition one step farther by offering bolt-on home office additions completely pre-wired for phone, fax, and coaxial modems or television. The company claims that once you have the foundation in, the office can be installed in a day. They offer a descriptive video.

gohome.com   If you have Yahoo, run a keyword search on "gohome.com" and you'll turn up links to about 200 (and growing) sites with some interest in working from home. Some are commercial, some are entrepreneurial, some are state organizations of home-based businesses or colleges and universities offering advice (how to set prices, for example), and some are just plain screwy. If you open the specific Web site "gohome.com," you'll be on the page for *Business@Home* magazine.

homeworks.com   This is the Web page of Paul and Sarah Edwards, the best-known writers, lecturers, and personalities on home-based entrepreneurship. These busy folks manage the Working from Home Forum on CompuServe, have a program on the Home & Garden television cable network (you can hear audio clips from their television and radio programs on the Web site), and are prolific authors, lecturers, and columnists. This site allows you to get a taste of all their activities.

pricecosto.com   News about small and home business issues from the *Christian Science Monitor* and *Business@Home* magazines are among the business services on the PriceCostco Web page's Small Business Zone. Other points of interest are an Idea Cafe that includes a form for budgeting your first year of operation, links to many small business resources, and words of wisdom from a consulting futurist on small and home business issues. It's friendly to use and not as commercial as one might expect.

smalloffice.com   *Home Office Computing* is an excellent magazine that covers much more than computing. It focuses on all aspects of the home-based business from legal to marketing and more. This is one of its online venues (the other is *soho@aol.com*) and it is a good place to start your research on any topic about running your business. It has organized articles from back issues into archives that can be searched by category (money, business, marketing, government, technology, etc.) or by key word. Articles range from a ranking of cities in which to start a small business to how to write a press release. You can download shareware, catch up on news, and check your weekly business horoscope, among other things. This represents what a Web site should be: easy and useful.

Topic: Jobs/Employment

monster.com   The monster board claims to list more than 50,000 jobs from 7,000 domestic and 1,500 international employers. It also allows you to search for contract or part-time work. You can choose your preferred city, state, or country and select from a directory of job titles or search by key word. There are daily newsgroup job postings and you can fill out a personal profile and send it to "Jobba the Hunt," who will return matching jobs to your in-box. If you're planning to relocate, here's a place to check the market at your destination. Or, with luck, you could pick up contract work in your own backyard.

natss.com/staffing   If working as a freelance temporary employee appeals to you, try this home page of the National Association of Temporary and Staffing Services, the trade organization for temporary service businesses. Increasingly, these jobs are for professionals in accounting, marketing, health care, and consulting. This Web site includes tips for job seekers, information on what to expect, and the ability to search for local members of the association by city or company name, including international locations. Many local offices have their own Web pages (or pages furnished by their national headquarters) and you can jump to those. In some cases, these local Web pages will contain specific current job listings.

Topic: Products and Services

bizweb.com   So, suppose you're interested in information about a product or service. How do you find out if the company has a Web page? This is a good place to start. BizWeb is a directory, a yellow pages of the Internet. It provides hot links to the Web pages of about 19,000 companies in 180 categories. You can scan through the categories or search by key words. It is a great equalizer of businesses, because General Motors gets no bigger listing than a guy at the corner garage who happens to have a Web site. Not everyone is listed here (I couldn't find BMW), but it is a very rich directory. It also flags which Web pages are new or updated within the past 30 days.

Topic: Travel

travelnow.com   Make airline and hotel reservations on the spot. Check availability and prices at 20,000 hotel properties in 5,000 cities worldwide, with 8,000 offering discounts up to 40 percent. For hotels, you identify your destination from a world map. For airlines, you open an account with a password, your own profile of travel preferences, and home airport.

vtourist.com   The Virtual Tourist site has two offerings. One is a directory of all the WWW servers in the world. Beginning with a map of the world, you click on choices that narrow your search to specific Web pages. You also have access to City.Net, for scoping out travel information for specific cities.

usair.com   All the major airlines have sites to inform you about their schedules, new deals for frequent flyer points, company news, and so on. Some (United is one) link you to other Web sites with restaurant or travel guides. USAir has a nice twist by allowing you to subscribe to a free weekly (Wednesday) e-mail alert of current discount flights. It's called E-savers. Plan to enter your e-mail address and, optionally, your frequent flyer number if you have one.

A few other airline addresses:

- American: americanair.com
- Continental: flycontinental.com
- Delta: delta-air.com
- Northwest: nwa.com
- United: ual.com

Topic: Business Details

usps.gov   Just about everything you need to know about mailing—from zip codes to domestic and international postage rates—is in this U.S. Postal Service Web offering. Tips on improving your mail handling, consumer news, a post office locator, and information on stamp collecting is here. So is information on passports, and a link to the Internal Revenue Service Web site (irs.gov), where you can find tax information, publications, and forms.

Topic: News

enews.com   Browse headlines and read portions of more than 2,000 magazines. Search by key words, create a profile to get just the topics you want e-mailed, and, of course, find opportunities to subscribe.

newspage.com   Newspage is a source for daily business news from 600 information sources. You can choose by topic, search by key words, or have a custom page set up to match your interests.

Topic: Mobile Products

You can find additional related sites in Chapter 11 on the mobile office.

mot.com   This is Motorola's Web site for cellular phones, pagers, modems, PC cards, wireless computing, and services. It provides a good overview of what's available and what's new from one of the leaders, and is handy for comparison shopping.

nokia.com   Based in Helsinki, Finland, Nokia is the world's second largest manufacturer of cellular phones and has a factory in Fort Worth, Texas. Nokia definitely takes a world view and this site provides a lot of information for international travelers through its Nokia Club (click Highlights/Nokia Club).

Product information, some with downloadable video clips and demos, is here, too.

Online Catalogs

These retailers are focused on slightly different aspects of the mobile communications universe.

themoo.com   The Mobile Office Outfitter offers a lot of gear to help set up your mobile workplace efficiently—car seat desks, trunk files, and so on, plus cellular and laptop accessories.

mplanet.com   MobilePlanet sells laptop computers as well as accessories, and offers detailed specs and photos of the laptops and other gear.

warrior.com   The Road Warrior Outpost sells equipment and accessories for mobile professionals, but it is very low key about it. This site offers a lot of information (for example, how to hook things up) in its library and has hot links to a variety of travel-related sites and listings of publications. If you poke around, you'll find a list of conferences and seminars on wireless communications technology. It's easy, informative, and offers an e-mail newsletter.

Topic: Government and Business

business.gov/ and sba.gov   These two sites provide information on how to do business with the federal government and its specific agencies, some regulations, and frequently asked questions. The *business.gov/* address will link you to the small business administration (SBA) site. By home business standards, the government's definition of small businesses is still pretty darned big. The SBA has a lot of information available for various kinds of businesses, and even lists its press releases. Perhaps most valuable is the information on programs for minority- and women-owned businesses, and its online version of a newsletter advocating small business found at: *sba.gov/advo/news/*. I've always wondered, though, why experts in small business are working in the federal bureaucracy.

yahoo.com/government/ This big chunk of the Yahoo browser provides a directory of government agencies, documents, and more than you ever wanted to know about all kinds of government topics from the military to judicial to the states.

whcsb.org Back in 1995, 2,000 delegates from small business went to the White House Conference on Small Business and made a wide range of recommendations for legislation that would improve the lot of small business. Much of it related to taxes, including the home office deduction. This Web site is supposed to provide an update on government action on those recommendations. A useful idea for tracking legislation, but when I visited this site two years later all the information was at least six months old. There were some promises that it soon would be fully operational, so by now it may be worth another visit.

Topic: Telecommuting

gilgordon.com Gil E. Gordon is a leading authority and consultant on telecommuting and coauthor (with Marcia Kelly) of "Telecommuting: How to Make It Work For You and Your Company" (Prentice-Hall, Inc.). If you want the latest on telecommuting, case studies, and links to sites with similar interests, here's where to look for them.

telecommute.org The International Telework Association posts information about telecommuting, a calendar of events, a directory of chapters, links to other telework-related sites, and frequently asked questions on its Web page.

Appendix B

Organizations for Home-Based Businesses

A variety of products, including health insurance and auto insurance, are available through several associations that target the needs of home-based businesses and the businesses that sell to them. In addition, these associations offer business information, news, opportunities to network, and, in some cases, they even lobby for small business interests. Each organization charges an annual membership fee, usually around $50, but if you can save on insurance or other products by comparison shopping the cost could be worth it. Their Web sites have news of interest to micro businesses and details about the organization's member benefits.

American Association of Home-Based Businesses
P.O. Box 10023, Rockville, MD 20849
http://www.aahbb.org; or e-mail: aahbb@crosslink.net

Benefits include a bimonthly newsletter, a business tips publication, discounts on travel and legal services, and long-distance service discounts. The association has chapters in Washington, D.C., Maryland, northern Virginia, central Ohio, Connecticut, Colorado, and Florida.

American Home Business Association, Inc.
4505 S. Wasatch Blvd., Salt Lake City, UT 84124
800-664-2422
http://www.homebusiness.com

This organization has an annual fee plus monthly fees, and offers a weekly e-mail newsletter of advice from home business experts, a monthly print newsletter, a quarterly magazine, a reciprocal link for your Web page, health and life insurance, legal services, letterhead printing, and a variety of other products.

Home Office Association of America
909 Third Ave., Suite 999, New York, NY 10022
800-809-4622
http://www.hoaa.com

Benefits include group health insurance, monthly newsletter, and discounts on airfare, long-distance rates, and many other products. If you are interested in direct marketing, you may want to look into their CD-ROM software products for business-to-business or business-to-consumer marketing. The Web site offers several hot links to others in the home-based business universe.

Independent Business Alliance
P.O. Box 1945, Danbury, CT 06813
800-450-2422

Benefits include medical and disability insurances, financial services, business advice, and discounts on long-distance rates, travel, telecommunications services, and products like computer gear and stationery.

International Homeworkers Association (IHA)
1925 Pine Ave., Suite 9035, Niagara Falls, NY 14301
716-284-6387
http://www.homeworkers.com

One of the interesting parts of the IHA Web site is a listing of jobs available for people who work from home, ranging from graphic designers to home assembly. The listing is buried. Go to "IHA Newsletter," then scan down to the bottom of the news items into the job listings section. The group says its roots are in organized labor. It has branches in Canada and England. Benefits include group health insurance, a wholesale shopping club, member chats, forums and seminars, and "scam alerts."

National Association for the Self-Employed (NASE)
P.O. Box 612067, Dallas, TX 75261
800-232-6273
http://www.nase.org

With more than 320,000 members, NASE is one of the largest and oldest of the small business organizations. It actively lobbies for small and home-based business legislation, offers products ranging from advice to software to bookkeeping systems, and shops for the best insurance deals on a state or regional basis. Call the 800 number for information on their insurance offerings in your area. NASE also publishes a newsletter of small business advice and updates on legislation.

Small Office Home Office Association (SOHOA)
1765 Business Center Dr., Suite 100, Reston, VA 22090
Toll free 888-764-6211
http://www.sohoa.com

If you have a Mail Boxes Etc. (MBE) nearby you can pick up information there, because MBE is a driving force behind this organization and has set up SOHOA "corners" in 2,000 participating MBE locations. Benefits include a subscription to *Home Office Computing* magazine, the SOHOA newsletter, access to a variety of insurances and financial services, and discounts on everything from travel and rental cars to prescriptions and eyeglasses.

APPENDIX C

Starting Your Own Home-Based Business

> "... When the road not taken disappears /
> into the path of least resistance ..."
> —Mary Chapin Carpenter, "Hero in Your Own Hometown"

*I*f you are now considering striking off on your own, you are poised at the edge of an incredible adventure. This is the time to take stock and gather as much information as you can and to lay out a plan of action.

In the sections below you'll find:

- A summary of the four basic things every business must do, large or small
- A few of the hard lessons I've learned in making the transition from a company environment to self-employment
- A list of suggested actions to help you get the ball rolling. They are designed to help you determine whether there is a market for your business, take some tangible steps toward making it on your own, and assess your own preparedness in taking the big step
- A worksheet to help you put your financial situation in perspective

Some businesses are more suitable for home-based businesses than others. Here's a list of the types of work currently being done from home.

The Top Ten Home-Based Businesses

1. Business consulting and services
2. Computer services and programming
3. Financial consulting and services
4. Marketing and advertising
5. Medical practice and services
6. Graphic and visual arts
7. Public relations and publicity
8. Real estate
9. Writing
10. Independent sales

Source: Link Resources, Inc.

The Good News: Just Four Things to Do

The good news is this: There are just four things you must do to operate a successful business—whether you are IBM, GM, or one person working out of a closet. You'll find that the rest of the book is devoted to details about these important areas:

1. Find and bring in the business or work. (Marketing)
2. Do the work or create the product. (Making Money)
3. Send bills, pay bills, pay taxes, get paid, keep records. (Administration)
4. Stay organized. Stay out of trouble. Follow up with clients. (Planning)

These are important yardsticks when you make decisions about how to spend your time and how you allocate your money for tools and supplies.

Unless you've worked in marketing before, it is easy to underestimate the importance of marketing. Marketing and cash flow—the task of growing and sustaining your business—will very likely be your two biggest problem areas. Consultants may spend three hours marketing for every hour they bill. And the time to market hardest is when you are very busy, because inevitably you'll wake up one morning thinking you are still very busy, only to realize you don't have much to do and there is nothing coming in the pipeline. This can cause a "clung": a rush of terror to the heart that is nearly audible.

Reality Checks

Be thoughtful and careful as you prepare to step off on your own. Our popular culture tells us that you will achieve your dreams if you "just do it." News coverage of the home-based business movement tends to profile the success stories. These are only half the story. Plenty of people fail, and I have known bright, talented people who threw caution to the wind in pursuit of a dream, only to bring terrible consequences down upon themselves and their families. Much of this book has been devoted to troubleshooting home-based businesses. Following are nine dictums you may have heard before. They are true, and if you keep them in mind you will find success is in large part based on clearly understanding the situation.

1. It is hard to make money. To succeed, you must produce a product or service that can be sold on the open market. Look around at the number of tasks performed by people making a good living that simply could not be sold on the open market. The corporate structure is necessary, in many cases, to provide employment.
2. Good ideas are a dime a dozen. Success comes to those who have the discipline to focus their efforts to implement a good idea. People have said to me, in all seriousness, "I have a lot of good ideas. Why don't I just have you implement them?"
3. Starting out on your own will take longer and cost more than you ever believed possible.
4. You pay for everything yourself. Everything.
5. Marketing and cash flow will be your biggest problems.
6. Large corporations move at a glacial pace in responding to your proposals; government is slower.
7. "The peace which passes all understanding" for the self-employed is a big savings account and small debt load.

8. You will be frightened at times. There is an enormous range of tolerance for risk. Some people love to quest; others love to nest. When you've crossed your threshold it can be a difficult period until you're back on track. The difference in the tolerance level should be identified, discussed, and worked out well in advance with a spouse or other significant individuals in your life.
9. People accustomed to regular paychecks tend to live on anticipated income. You can't, at least not until you're well established, and even then it's risky.

Step-by-Step Toward Your Goal

There is never a perfect time to strike off on your own. Many home workers would still be in the corporate nest if they hadn't been nudged. People who start thinking seriously about going out on their own can be reduced to bowls of pudding by anxiety attacks.

The answer is to take little steps, not a giant headlong plunge. Here are 15 things you can do while gainfully employed that will move you in the right direction.

1. Conduct a sanity test. Thoroughly investigate whether or not there is a need for your business. Is there a market for it? How many people are already filling the need? Check the yellow pages. How are they *really* doing? In small communities, the business pie can be so small that one person can make a decent living, but three doing the same thing will struggle. People launching their own business fall in love with their ideas. Love is blind. If I had a dollar for every start-up who told me "I think we're really on to something here. This is big . . . ." I would be sailing in the Caribbean.

Writing a business plan is a good sanity test. It makes you think of and come to grips with those pesky issues that you choose to ignore when infatuated. People usually write business plans when they must go to the bank and borrow money. You may simply take out a personal loan for things, but the business plan process is a wonderful way to focus on your business idea and test its sanity. You can buy software designed for developing business plans. Often these programs will start a sentence and you must fill in the blanks: "The corporate mission of Laura's Live Bait and Beer Store is to . . . ."

To get the ball rolling, try writing your own marketing plan. You'll find an outline in the first section of this book.

2. Choose a target date or deadline. "Someday" will never come. After sorting through the items below, a reasonable date will probably surface. Allow enough time, and assign weekly and monthly deadlines for beginning and completing the steps that follow.

3. Open a separate checking account for your business. At tax time, it is much better if you have not slipped into the very bad habit of commingling your personal and business finances. This business checkbook should have one rule: Only write checks from it for business purposes. Once you are making money, you can write checks to yourself for your salary and enter them as a "draw." Beyond the practical aspects, a business checking account is the most tangible reminder that you are on your way.

4. Reduce your debt. Being a slave to credit cards or installment debt is risky to fatal for the self-employed. Do you own your possessions or do your possessions own you? To find out, complete the financial worksheet at the end of this chapter. If you must borrow, want to refinance your home, or decide to establish a home equity line of credit, you should do so while still employed. It can be very hard to borrow when your new business has no track record. Some brokerage accounts have borrowing, credit card, and check writing privileges.

5. Build up a cash reserve. Cash flow will always be a problem. It is frightening to dig into a cash reserve to cover shortfalls, but you can build it back up when the checks finally arrive. It is much worse not to have such a reserve and find you are afraid to answer the phone because the collection people are on your case. To get a handle on what you really need to carry you through slow periods, see the worksheet at the end of this chapter.

6. Create a "Board of Advisers." Ask friends or business acquaintances if they would be willing to join a group of informal advisers to act as mentors or consultants as you move toward your goal. Make sure they are discreet about your plans, or defer this step until you make your move. From time to time take the group out to dinner and go over your written agenda of issues and questions. Pick people who are strong in areas that you are weak in. Ask them where good information and essentials such as financing can be found. The most important function of this group could be "sanity testing" your business idea.

7. Build a prospect data base. You know a lot of people. Now start thinking of them as potential prospects for your business. Your suppliers in your job today may become your clients tomorrow. Round up all those business cards. Get the information into a computer. One of the first things you will do when you strike out on your own is write them each a personal letter announcing your plans and asking for their business or referrals.

8. Attend a conference or trade show in your area of business. Scout out what's being done and who is doing it. Is there a need for your product or service? Network. Collect business cards. In a subtle way, test your idea on the people who are likely to become your customers. Get a list of attendees. Put it into your database. Follow up with a note or card to your new contacts when you return home.

9. Acquire some business skills and tools. Set aside a war chest and begin acquiring the tools you will need. Take some classes in business and computer subjects. You'll meet potential business contacts there, too.

10. Create a "launch" file. Imagine the big day is here. You've written the "I'm afraid we've come to a fork in the road . . ." letter to your employer and have cleaned out the desk drawer. Now what? Well, you issue a press release. Draft it in advance and build a media list in your database. Send letters to everyone announcing your new business. Write it ahead of time and make sure you have a database of people who will get it. Get your letterhead and business card designed and ready to print.

You may run advertising—create it. You may have a brochure or sell sheet—write and design it. You will want to make appointments with people you have identified as promising clients or customers. Store their names and phone numbers using the "organizer" software in your computer for the big day. When you launch your business it is impossible to do too much. It is easy to do too little. Be prepared.

11. Look for an opportunity disguised as a problem. Having once worked for a company that was downsized and is now teetering at the edge of bankruptcy, I am well aware of the cloud of anxiety that hangs over many businesses today as they downsize and outsource work—possibly your work. This may, in fact, be the very thing you are looking for if you can cut a deal to leave the company but continue on as a supplier. It may not last forever, but it could ease the transition and allow you to fly off on your own, buying some time to get other business. So, don't burn bridges, build them. The truth is, it may be just the push you need to act on your plan. There will never be a perfect time to act on any life-altering endeavor.

12. Audit your benefits situation with your current employer. Since the passage of the Kassenbaum-Kennedy Health Insurance Reform Act in 1996 you can take your existing health insurance with you without preconditions (there used to be an 18-month limit), but you will pay for it and that can be very expensive. You will have choices to make between picking up the payments on the current policy and looking elsewhere. Also consider where you stand with your retirement package. Are you fully vested? Would it pay to wait? Sit down with a financial adviser to plan a clear path for your 401(k) funds, if you have them, into a rollover IRA. Typical choices are banks, mutual funds, or brokers, and there are many additional choices within each of those categories.

Get a physical and take care of medical needs while still covered by your employer.

13. Define success on your own terms for a change. "More" does not necessarily equal "better." This is your dream, so only you can live it. I would simply caution that you should define success by moving *toward* something, not just away from a bad situation. Try to describe what you are seeking. Sit down and list the three most important things that would be happening if your home business was working ideally.

Here's an example of one of the items from my list a few years back: "I would have a product that could generate a revenue stream independent of simply billing my time by the hour." You are holding it in your hand.

14. Practice yoga and learn to live with your fears.

15. Understand the reality of your specific needs. Taking a look at your own financial situation right now will do four things for you:

1. It will give you an idea of what you need or want to earn. Come back to this when you set your rates. There should be some correlation.
2. It will help identify how much you need in reserve to survive. Suppose you went for three months or six months without any business at all?
3. It will get you started on planning for the big expenses in life such as retirement and college tuition.
4. It will identify those costs you will pay when self-employed that you didn't pay before. This will probably take a few phone calls for items like insurance.

How Much Will I Need? Then and Now

Following is a worksheet that will help you understand your financial situation today and compare it with what it is likely to be when you have set off to make it on your own. It is a planning tool that takes a little time to fill out, but it is time well spent because you have so much at stake in making the right decision. It does not focus on your net worth, which is typical of loan applications. Instead, it focuses on your cash flow needs. When you do not receive a paycheck on a regular schedule, your ability to plan for income fluctuations is critical to your survival. You can use the same worksheet to evaluate your retirement prospects, decide whether or not to take a company buyout, or find out if you can afford to take a six-month sabbatical to consider how you want to spend the rest of your life.

The worksheet is fairly easy and can be completed by referring to your checkbook to see how much you spend each month in the various categories. Some items such as insurances may be paid quarterly or annually, so simply break the payments down into months. If you currently use one of the checkbook computer programs like Quicken or Mind Your Own Business, you can create this worksheet as a "custom report" and the program will handle all the math. Then you can update it whenever you need to do some financial planning.

The worksheet is broken into two kinds of expenses: fixed expenses and flexible expenses. Fixed expenses are long-term commitments. Flexible expenses are the areas where you have choices about how much you spend.

I've built in "now" and "then" columns to help identify what may change or where you can make changes. Four main questions need to be answered: What do I have? What do I need? What can I change? And, of course: Can I pull it off?

Items likely to have a greater significance when you are on your own will be followed by one or more + or – signs, depending on their impact. Some will cost more, some less. An * means this is something new to think about.

Financial Worksheets

Monthly Fixed Expenses	Now	Then
Mortgage/rent		
Utilities		
Electricity		
Oil/Gas		
Condo Fees		
Home Telephone		
Insurance		
Life+		
Disability++		
Automobile		
Homeowners		
Liability+		
Medical+++		
Taxes		
Real Estate		
Estimated Federal*		
Estimated State		
Personal Property		
Self-Employment*		
Debt		
Auto #1		
Auto #2		
Big Toys		
Education		
Credit Card #1		
Credit Card #2		
Credit Card #3		
Other		
Alimony/Child Support		
Total Fixed Expenses		

Financial Worksheets (Continued)

Monthly Flexible Expenses	Now	Then
Food		
Groceries		
At Work		
Dining Out		
Liquor/Wine		
Clothing		
Husband		
Wife		
Children		
Personal Care		
(haircuts, cosmetics, etc.)		
Home Maintenance		
Yard & Garden		
Repairs		
Snow Removal		
Trash Removal		
Services (bugs, cleaning, etc.)		
Renovations		
Decorating		
Small Stuff		
Transportation		
Gas/Oil		
Repairs		
Maintenance		
Commuting⁻		
Parking⁻		
Registration		
Pet Expenses		
Subscriptions and dues*+		

Financial Worksheets (Continued)

Monthly Flexible Expenses	Now	Then
Children		
Child care		
Sitters		
Classes		
Recreation		
Entertainment		
Sports & Recreation		
Vacations		
Education		
Tuition		
Room & Board		
Books, etc.		
Travel		
Spending Money		
Medical		
Doctor		
Dentist		
Mental Health		
Prescriptions		
Home Office*++		
Telephone		
Computer		
Fax		
Postage		
Supplies		
Furniture		
Equipment		
Advertising		
Internet/Online Services		
Legal Fees		
Accountant		

Financial Worksheets (Continued)

Monthly Flexible Expenses	Now	Then
Contract labor		
Business Travel		
Cellular		
Pagers/Telecom Services		
Retirement Plan Contribution++		
Total Monthly Flexible Expenses		

Now consider your ability to sustain yourself over rough periods. Could you live for six months by drawing on the following?

Sources of Emergency Income

Monthly Savings and Set-Asides from Work (401(k), payroll savings, other savings plans) Husband _____ Wife _____ *Total Now Available* _____	
Emergency Fund	_____

Savings accounts
    Available
    Earmarked (for college tuition, etc.)
	_____
	 _____

Investments (stocks, bonds, money market funds, etc.)
    Available cash
    Penalty cash (IRAs, retirement plans
    if used before age 59½)
	_____
	 _____

Other	_____
Non-Salary, Non-Business Income (Rentals, etc.)	_____
Second Income	_____
Total Available:	_____

And Think About . . .

The cost and availability of insurances, particularly disability insurance, is worth investigating before you take off. Don't just gloss over it. You may save money by getting into a business or professional group, like a chamber of commerce or work-at-home membership organization. Having one member of the family provide health care coverage for all by working in mainstream America is a real blessing.

Now you also will be paying estimated quarterly income taxes instead of having them deducted in advance, so only about two-thirds of the money you receive from the business should be considered as "yours." If you earn $40,000, you will probably be in the 28 percent tax bracket and will have to come up with roughly 28 percent of your estimated annual income to pay in installments on the 15th of April, June, September, and January. This can create some unpleasant surprises until you get used to it, particularly in April when you pay any balance due on last year's income tax *plus* a quarterly estimate. If you work with your accountant, this should become routine.

Finally, you now have to pay for your own retirement plan through an IRA or Keogh Plan. Money you pull out of your 401(k) and other company-provided plans can be sheltered from taxes by putting them into a "rollover" plan. Do not park rollover money in a personal checking account even temporarily or it will be disqualified as a rollover. Move it directly into a qualified retirement plan. IRA and Keogh plans provide you the opportunity to deduct your retirement contribution from your income before it is computed for tax purposes. IRAs are easy to set up through financial institutions and brokers. There is a penalty for taking money out of the plans before you reach age 59½, so these funds should not be viewed as "rainy day" funds unless the day is very rainy indeed. When you take money out of these accounts it is taxed as income. Your financial adviser may be able to help you choose the plan that is best for you.

INDEX

A

aboutwork.com, 162-63
Action plan and timetable, in proposal, 67
Administration, 173
Advertising, 14, 38-39, 46, 78, 173
  strategy, 106
Agreements, 70, 72-75
AIDA, 24-25
Airborne Express, 141
Airline internet addresses, 165-66
Ambient lighting, 119
American Association of Home-Based Businesses, 160, 169
American Home Business Association, Inc., 169-70
AOL, 151
Appearance, personal, 36
Apple (Newton), 150
ARDIS, 151
AT&T PersonalLink, 151
AT&T Wireless, 151
Attachments, included in proposal, 68-69
Attention, 24
Auto expenses, 78
  deduction for, 99

B

Bacon's Directories, 53
Balance sheets, 106
Bankcard Holders of America, 95
Barker, Joel, 153
Benefits, 178
  for temporary workers, 136-37
Berra, Yogi, 1
Billing cycles, 85
BIS Strategic Decisions, 160
bizweb.com, 165
Board of advisers, 177
Boggs, Raymond, xi, 156-57
Booklets, 59
bradyrooms.com, 163
Breakeven analysis, 107
Brochures, 39
Budget, 107
  in proposal, 68
Burgess, Phil, 137-38
Business cards, 35
Business climate, 140
Business consulting and services, 173
Business deductions, 99-100
Business description, 106
Business plans, 2-3
  financing and, 106-8
Business skills, 177

Index   **187**

Business telephone line, 126-28
business.gov, 167
Business@Home magazine, 163
By the project billing, 84

C

Calendar, marketing, 13
Canon Computer Systems, 146
Canon USA, 160
Capital equipment list, 106
Card file, 19
CardTrak, 94
CardWeb, 94
Carpenter, Mary Chapin, 172
Cash flow, 14, 173, 174
Cash reserve, 176
Casio, 150
Casting, 22-23
Celente, Gerald, 137, 154
Cellular phone, 147, 148
Center for the New West, 138
Checkbook computer programs, 180
Checking account, business, 176
Christian Science Monitor, 163
Citizen America Corp., 146
City.Net, 165
Client
    payment system of, understanding, 70-71
    relations, 35
Client files, 120
Climate, for business, 140-41
COBRA, 92-93, 100
Cold calling, 14, 15, 16, 43-44
Collection
    agencies, 89
    on slow payments, 86-88
Commerce on the Net, 155
Communication, AIDA, 24-25
Communications specialists, 145-46
Community development, 105
Competition, 11
Competitive analysis, 106

Complete Guide to Consulting Contracts, The, 74
CompuServe, 151
Computer checkbook, 98
Computer equipment
    deduction for, 99
    home-based business and, 18-19
Computer services and programming, 173
Condominiums, and home businesses, 110
Conferences, 31, 177
Consulting, 173
Consumer protection agencies, 88, 89, 95
Contact management programs, 19
Container Store, The, 124
Contingency work, 85
"Contract creep," 71
Contract employees, 136
Country Bound! Trade Your Business Suit Blues for Blue Jean Dreams, 142
Courier services, 141
Credibility, 23, 31
Credit card
    costs, 94-95
    debt, 109
Customer(s)
    importance of multiple, 26
    motivation, 23-24

D

Damart, 148
Database, 50, 177
    programs, 19
    prospect, 32
Deadlines, 7, 176
Debt reduction, 176
Deferred billing, 85
Deferred taxes, 101-2
Deliverables, in proposal, 68
Direct mail, 13-14, 40-41, 46
    seminars and, 45
Disability insurance, 78, 93, 180

188　　　　　　　　　　　　Index

Discipline, 30
Downsizing
　by clients, 11
　by employer, 157, 178

E

E-mail-back, 129
E-savers, 165
Editor and Publisher Yearbook, 53
Editorial calendars, 14
Education, 177
Edwards, Paul and Sarah, 163
800 and 888 numbers, 130
Electronic filing cabinet, 19
Emergency funds, 134
Emergency income, 185
Employees, 111-12
Employment internet addresses, 164
enews.com, 166
Entertainment, 78, 99
Equipment, in homeowners
　insurance, 92
Estimated income taxes, 100-101
eWorld, 151
Executive summary, 106
Exercise, 9

F

Face-to-face business relationships,
　15, 31
Fair debt collection laws, 88, 89
Falvey, Jack, 33
Fax-back, 128-29
Federal Express, 141
Fees. *See* Rates, for services
Files, 120, 121, 123, 125
Financial consulting and services,
　173
Financial worksheets, 180, 182-85
Financing, 103-9
　business plans and, 106-8
　sources of, 104-5, 108-9
Find/SVP Research, 159
500 numbers, 130
Fixed fees or retainers, 84

Flat rate billing, 84
Follow-up activities, 173
　to leads, 37
　to marketing efforts, 14
　to press kits, 58
Forbes, Malcom, 76
Franklin, Benjamin, 10
Fraud, 95
Furniture manufacturer, 124, 126
Futurists, 154-56

G

gilgordon.com, 168
Global market, 155
Goal(s)
　achievement, 175-79
　setting, 3, 156
gohome.com, 163
Gordon, Gil E., 158-59, 168
Gould, Jay, 91
Government contracts, 63, 80
Government Internet addresses, 167
Graphic arts, 173
Group insurance, 94

H

Half day billing, 83-84
Health insurance, 91, 92-93, 178
　premiums, deductions for, 100
　temporary workers and, 137
Health maintenance organizations,
　93, 140
Hello Direct, 128
Herman Miller, 124
Hewlett-Packard, 146, 150
Hiemstra, Glen, 154-56
HMOs, 93, 140
Hold Everything, 124
Holtz, Herman, 74
Home equity line of credit, 176
Home equity loans, 109
Home Office Association of
　America, 170
Home Office Computing magazine,
　18, 142, 146, 160, 164, 171

Index

Home Office Computing Web site, 74
Home office deduction, 95–98
Home Office Research Program, 156
Home worker profile, 159–60
Home-based businesses, top ten, 173
Home-based business plan, 3–8
   goals and, 4–8
Homeowners insurance, 92
homeworks.com, 163
Hoteling, 144. *See also* Mobile office
Hourly rates, establishing, 77–80. *See also* Rates, for services

I

IDC/Link, x, xi, 156, 159, 160
Improvements to land, 113
Income
   determining amount needed, 179–80
   sources of emergency, 185
Income statement, 106
Income taxes
   estimated, 100–101
   quarterly, 180
Independent Business Alliance, 170
Independent sales, 173
Infinity, Limited, 153
Insurance, 78, 91–94, 180
   disability, 78, 93, 180
   group, 94
   health, 91, 92–93, 100, 137, 178
   HMOs, 93, 140
   policies, as sources of financing, 109
Integrated Services Digital Network, 130–31
Interest, 24
INTERMARK, 33
Internal Revenue Service Web site, 166
International Homeworkers Association, 170
International Telework Association, 168
Internet, 32, 41–42, 147
   addresses, 161–68
      business details, 166
      domains, 161–62
      government and business, 167–68
      jobs and employment, 164
      mobile products, 166–67
      news, 166
      online catalogs, 167
      products and services, 165
      self-employment and working from home topics, 162–64
      telecommuting, 168
      travel, 165–66
Invoices, 82
IRA, 181
irs.gov, 166
ISDN, 130–31

J–K

Job Internet addresses, 164
Kassenbaum-Kennedy Health Insurance Reform Act, 178
Keogh Plan, 102, 181
Keough, Kate, 116, 121
Knoll, 126

L

Labels, 19
Launch file, 177
Leacock, Stephen, 29
Leadership Library 1.0, 154
Leading your client, 35
Leads, follow-up of, 37
Legal advice, 74–75
Letter of agreement, 70, 72–75
Letterheads, 35, 39
Letters, personal, 41
Lewis, Joe E., 103
Liaison Cabinet System, 126

Lifespan, 155
Lighting, for home office, 119
Lines of credit, 109
Link Resources, x
Listening skills, 35, 37
Loans. *See* Financing
Long-distance rates, 94
Lotus 1-2-3, 151

M

Mail Boxes Etc., 145, 171
Mail Remote, 151
Mailings, promotional, 13-14. *See also* Direct mail
Mannesmann Tally Corp., 146
Market Extension Line, 126
Marketing, 173-74. *See also* Public relations
    AIDA, 24-25
    arrows, 38-39, 47
    calendar, 13, 17
    customer motivation and, 23-24
    evaluating, 11-13
    follow-up activities and, 14
    habits, 30-38
    new prospects and, 32-35
    package, 39
    problems, 25
    research, 106
    strategies, 22-23
    telephone, 43-44
    troubleshooting, 27-28
Mass mailings. *See* Direct mail
MCI, 151
Meal deductions, 99
Medical expense deductions, 99
Medical practice and services, 173
Meetings, 15
    preparation for, 33-35
    proposals and, 64-65
Micro loan programs, 104, 107-8
Microsoft Windows CE, 150
Microsoft Works, 151
Midstream changes, 71
Milestones, 6

Mind Your Own Business, 107, 180
Mobile office, 144-60
    cellular phones, 147, 148
    notebook computers and portable printers, 146, 148
    pagers, 149
    personal communications services, 151
    personal digital assistants, 150-51
Mobile Office magazine, 146, 147
Mobile Office Outfitter, 167
Mobile Planet, 167
Mobile products Internet addresses, 166-67
MobileComm, 149
Modern Postcard, 40
Money management software, 107
monster.com, 164
Moonlighting, 135-36
mot.com, 166
Motorola, 150, 166
mplanet.com, 167

N

National Association for the Self-Employed, 95, 171
National Association of Temporary and Staffing Services, 135, 164
National Foundation for Women Business Owners, 159
natss.com/staffing, 164
Networking, 19, 177
Net worth statement, 107
News, on the internet, 166
Newsletters, 39-40
newspage.com, 166
Newspaper "morgue," 90
nokia.com, 167
Non-profit organizations, 84
Nonresidential use of property, 113-14
Notebook computer, 148
Notecards, 41
Notetaking, during client meetings, 33
Novello, Don, 133

Index

O

Objectives, in proposal, 66
Occupational Outlook Handbook, 78
Occupational Safety and Health Act, 111
Office efficiency, 116-20
Online catalogs, 167
Online information services, 139, 147
Opportunities, 12
Organization, 19, 115-32, 173
    of telecommunications, 126-32
    office efficiency, 116-20
    space needs, 121-26
Organizations, 169-71
Organizer programs, 19
Outlook, for home-based businesses, 153-60
Outsourcing, 157
Overhead, 78-79

P-Q

PageMart, 149
PageNet, 149
PageNet StarLink, 151
Partnering, 11, 42-43
Payment for services
    collecting from slow clients, 86-90
    determining, 63-64, 77-80
    discounting, 69-70, 84
    method for, 83-85
    methods of billing, 83-85
    terms of, in letter of agreement, 74
Payment system, of client, 70-71
PC World, 146
PC-based answering systems, 129
Pentax Technologies, 146
Personal communications services, 151
Personal digital assistant, 150-51
Phantom phone number, 129-30
Photos, in press kit, 57
Physical activity, 9

Piece rate billing, 85
Place (location), 27
Planning, 173
Plan of operation, 106
Pocket Quicken, 151
Popcorn, Faith, 153
Portable printers, 146
Positioning, 27
Postcards, 20, 40. *See also* Direct mail
Power inverter, 148
Press kit, 56-58
Press list, 50-53
Press release, 41, 51, 53-55
Price, 27, 28. *See also* Payment for services
pricecosto.com, 163
Printers, portable, 146
Product, 27, 28
Production/communication area, 115, 119
Production/storage space, 119
Products and services, Internet addresses for, 165
Professional societies, and sample letters of agreement, 73
Profile, of home worker, 159-60
Promotion, 27
    strategy, 106
Proposal(s), 61-71
    answering unasked client questions, 62-63
    developing, 33
    developing a price, 63-64
    meetings and, 64-65
    partners and, 43
    sample outline, 65-69
    troubleshooting, 69-71
Prospect database, 32, 177
Prospects
    frequency of contact with, 24-25
    mailings to, 20
    organization of, 16-22
Public access, 113
Publicity, 13-14, 46, 173. *See also* Direct mail; Public relations

Public relations, 47–60, 173
    press kit, 56–58
    press list, 50–53
    press release, 53–55
    publicity placements, 59–60
    purpose of, 49–50
    story pitch, 58–59
Quality of life, 141
Quicken, 107, 151, 180

R

RadioMail, 151
Ram Research Web site, 94
Rates, for services
    collecting from slow clients, 85–90
    determining, 63–64
    discounting, 69–70, 84
    method for, 83–85
    terms of, in letter of agreement, 74
Real estate, 173
Recordkeeping, 98–101
Referrals, pursuing, 31
Relationships, face-to-face, 31
Reliable Home Office, 124
Relocating, 137–43
"Remote control" selling, 32
Resume, 107
Retirement plan(s), 78, 101–2, 178, 181
    deductions, 99–100
Retirement trends, 155
Revolving loan funds, 105
Ringmate, 128
Road warrior, 144. *See also* Mobile office
Road Warrior Outpost, 167
Rollover (retirement) plan, 181

S

Salary Reduction SEP, 102
Sales, independent, 173
SAR-SEP, 102
Savings Incentive Match Plan for Employees, 102
sba.gov, 167
Scams, 95
Schaefer, David, 47
School & Home Office Products Association, 160
Seasonal fluctuations, 26
Self-employment tax, 78
Self-management, 156
Self-promotion, 31
Seminars, 31, 45–46
SEP-IRA, 101–2
Setbacks vs. catastrophes, 134–35
    MicroLoan Program, 107
Sharp, 150
SIMPLE, 102
Situation analysis, in proposal, 65
Sky-Tel, 149
Small Business Administration, 104
    loans, 108
Small Business Development Center, 104
Small claims court, 88–89
Small Office Home Office Association (SOHOA), 171
smalloffice.com, 164
Social Security, 101–2
Software, 18–19, 107
SOHOA newsletter, 171
Soliman, Nader, 95–96
Sony, 150
Space planning, 116–20
Special events, 45–46
Speculative work, 85
Sprint, 151
Start-up businesses, problems with, 25
Steelcase, 126
Storage, 116–17, 119–20, 121–26
Story pitch, 58–59
Strategic Leadership: Achieving Your Preferred Future, 154
Subcontracting, 76
Sutton, Willie, 138

Index

T

Target date, 176
Task lighting, 119
Tax deductions, 95-98
    recordkeeping and, 98-101
Tax forms, for unincorporated independent contractors, 112
Tax returns, 107
Techline, 124
Technotribalism, 137
Telecommunications, organization of, 126-32
telecommute.org, 168
Telecommuting, 158-59
    Internet addresses for, 168
Telecommuting—How to Make it Work for You, 158
telegroup.com, 94
Telephone
    costs, 94
    deduction for, 99
    services, 128-31
    system, 36
Telephone marketing, 43-44
Temporary work and services, 111-12, 135-37
themoo.com, 167
Third Wave, The, 153
Thurber, James, 153
Timing, 39
Toffler, Alvin, 153
Trade magazines, 51, 53
Trade shows, 177
Training, 135-36, 177
Travel expenses, 78, 81, 99
trasvelnow.com, 165
Travel topic Internet addresses, 165
Trends Research Institute, 137, 154
Trends, for home-based businesses, 153-60
Trolling, 22-23
Troubleshooting, 27-28

U

U.S. Department of Labor, 112
U.S. Postal Service Web site, 166
Unincorporated independent contractors, 112
Unique Selling Proposition, 36-37, 39
United Airlines, 165
UPS, 141
usair.com, 165
usps.gov, 166

V

Vacation deductions, 99
Video conferencing, 131
Video production, 82
Virtual company, 131-32
Virtual Tourist, The, 165
Visibility, increasing, 23
Visual arts, 173
vtourist.com, 165

W

Warriner, William, 61, 115
warrior.com, 167
Web sites, 41-42
whcsb.org, 168
White House Conference on Small Business, 112
Wood, Lyman, ix, 46
Work-linking, 42-43
Work zones, 116-20
Working from Home Forum, 163
Working Press of the Nation, 53
Worksheets, financial, 180, 182-85
Workshops, 45-46
Writing, 173

Y-Z

yahoo.com/government/, 168
Yellow pages, 36
Yoga, 179
"Your Personal Earnings and Benefit Estimate Statement," 102
Zoning, 110-11
    public access and, 113

Cable & Wireless Has Your Number!

Cable & Wireless, Inc. understands your home-based business. Keeping your eye on expenses. Constantly monitoring cash flow. Staying in touch with customers.

Cable & Wireless custom designs long distance solutions to make you the best in your business. You can receive a FREE telecom consultation from Cable & Wireless to help you increase productivity, decrease operating costs, and gain a competitive edge.

**Cable & Wireless has your number.
Because in your business, numbers count.**

For a FREE Telecom Consultation
and 30% off our regular rates

Call 1-800-969-1029
and ask for Eileen Barnicle.

CABLE & WIRELESS, INC.